DAUGHTER'S CHOICE

"A CHILD'S NIGHTMARE OF GROWING UP IN THE FOSTER CARE SYSTEM AND HOW THE SYSTEM FAILED TO PROTECT HER."

DIANNA HOLDEN

DAUGHTER'S CHOICE
A Worldwide People Locators Publishing Book

Published by
Worldwide People Locators Publishing
A Division of 0845450 BC LTD
Abbotsford, British Columbia Canada

ISBN 978-0-9864896-3-1
http://www.worldwidepeoplelocators.com

For all the foster children who have never been heard
···

Your words count···. Now it is time for people to listen···.

Abuse in foster care "NEEDS TO STOP" and Child Protection Agencies need to be held accountable···

Criminally for their actions···

Worldwide···

Introduction

The subject matter that you are about to read may be considered graphic and disturbing to the reader as it discusses physical, sexual, and emotional abuse of children, while residing under the care of a system that is set up to protect them. The story which is based on a true account of growing up in the foster care system in British Columbia Canada, addresses wide span issues that occur throughout most child protection agencies. The story provides the reader a true account of what happens to some children who end up being thrust into the Foster Care System, and of children who end up in the Youth Detention Centers.

I have utilized pseudonyms for the names of anyone where legislation prevents, the naming of the individual being identified such as other children that were in care, as well as others that were inmates under the young offenders act. I have done this to ensure that I am adhering to the legislation of Privacy. Any names that are similar to that of an individual in real life, is purely coincidental.

There are many books out there that tell you how this happened and that happened in foster care, but have you ever read a book that not only addresses the issues of a government system that has failed our children but offers possible solutions to those issues. This is exactly what "Daughter's Choice", is all about, offering solutions to our failing Child Protection System(s).

This book was extremely emotionally draining to write, as I am the girl that is the main character of this story. I thought long and hard as to whether or not I should write in a pseudonym name for myself, but regardless if I had, someone, somewhere, out there will always have an opinion about the contents of this book. I am not ashamed of who I am or where I have come from. I have not followed societies stereotype of what happens to children who are out of the foster care system. All too often, it's the child grew up in care that is penalized because they are labeled the bad children of society. Although statistics show that many children that grow up in government care do not follow through on their education, or get into upper class occupations, not all children fall into this category. While writing this book I utilized the information I received under the Freedom of Information Act to compile many of the situations that are outlined in the story, so that I was not relying on memory alone.

Some of the conversations and interviews have been re-created from the original transcripts from social services records. For the portions relating to the time that I was placed in the Youth Detention Center, and the Maples Adolescent Treatment Center. I have recreated situations from documents received under the Freedom of Information & Privacy Act.

I have utilized pseudonyms for the names of my abusers, my parents, my sibling, as well as any child that was in the foster care system and youth detention center with me. The background history, and the character descriptions are completely fictitious, to protect those individuals. Should the names and identifiable information be similar to a live person it is purely coincidental.

This piece of literature was not written to judge the Province of British Columbia's Youth Justice System, or the Foster Care System, but to create awareness that without changes being made, both systems are failing our children. It was also written to suggest solutions to the ever-growing issues that people involved with the Foster Care System face.

All too often children whom are apprehended and thrust into the Child Protection System are not believed when they make allegations of abuse in the facilities, which the Child Protection Agencies utilize. Children in care need to be heard. There needs to be accountability when it comes to the Social Workers whom leave these children in abusive foster homes, or privately run contracted facilities.

Thank you for taking the time to read this book I hope that you enjoy it.

Disclaimer: The opinions, and ideas expressed in this book are not necessarily the opinions and ideas of the Canadian Foster Family Association or the BC Federation of Foster Parents.

Regards

Dianna Holden

Chapter 1
"Medical Apprehension"

The spring of 1974, was a tough one for 24-year-old Jasmine Johnson & 36-year-old Hunter Davidson. Jasmine, a stay at home mom, of an almost two-year-old Laura Lee, was 26 weeks pregnant with her second child. Jasmine, loved being pregnant however, this pregnancy was much different from her first, as she did not seem to be gaining very much weight during her pregnancy. Standing five foot six, entering her third trimester she thought she would be larger than she was, after all she only gained 5 pounds. Regardless of the lack of weight gain, they were ecstatic that a new baby would be arriving.

Jasmine, met Hunter while he was working at the local hotel pub, she thought he was handsome. Hunter twelve years her senior, stood six foot four weighing two hundred and ten pounds wore his hair neat and short. He was what society would call buff. Regardless of the age difference, Jasmine was in love.

Although the first two years together had been rough with all the moves and lack of stable employment for Hunter, Jasmine felt the new baby would change things. Hunter would perhaps stop drinking, and be more involved with Laura-Lee and the new baby and have more of an incentive to find full time work.

Unknown to Jasmine or Hunter was that their little baby had decided to enter the world much earlier than expected and would cause a huge rift between a mother and father and a government agency.

On the morning of the 13 of April 1974, just as Jasmine was preparing breakfast for Laura Lee, she started getting contractions. Thinking it was Braxton Hicks a nickname given when pregnant woman think they are in true labor because their body is contracting, but they are not in actual labor, she continued cooking. As Jasmine was leaning over to grab the toast from the toaster, her water broke. Trying not to panic Jasmine swiftly grabbed the telephone that was hanging on the wall and called the neighbor to come watch Laura-Lee and to take her to the hospital. Darlene a woman in her early forties, who was Jasmine & Hunters neighbor quickly arrived, and bustled Laura-Lee into her car seat and raced off to the Vancouver General Hospital with Jasmine in labor in the front passenger seat.

At the hospital, Jasmine was rushed to the maternity area, and they prepped for her to have the baby. Putting together a team of doctors and nurses, was a tedious task for the hospital staff, as they had never had a baby born at 26 weeks gestation before, and they were unsure as to what to expect.

At 11:10 am, a very sick baby was born; "ME". The baby, named by Jasmine as Dianna weighed 1 lb 13 oz. and was the smallest baby that had ever been born in the hospital. It was at that point that the hospital realized I was so sick that I would require extensive surgeries, and medical care to survive.

Jasmine frantically tried to get a hold of my dad Hunter, eventually tracking him down at the local pub. Jasmine filled my father in on the details that I had been born. She also told him that she was at the Children's Hospital, and that my sister was at the neighbors. Hunter highly intoxicated quickly attended the hospital only to be quickly re-directed by the nursing staff to go home until he sobered up.

I was transferred to the Intensive Care unit under the care of pediatric surgeon Dr. Graham Fraser, a very mild mannered man that was excellent at what he did. Dr. Fraser was from Britain and was a fantastic surgeon. Dr. Fraser, was the chief pediatric surgeon at BC Children's Hospital. Although Dr. Fraser did not work alone in saving my life, I credit him with all his hard work and dedication. Dr. Fraser made my life possible and without his medical expertise, I would not be alive today. For this, I am so grateful. Just to give an idea as to what my medical problems entailed. I was born with an esophageal atresia without a fistula, meaning that my esophagus failed to develop into a continuous passageway; instead, it stopped into a blind pouch.

I had to have a tracheotomy; I had mal-absorption of the bowels, as well as a bowel blockage which created bowel movements out my mouth as well as constant diarrhea. Due to my extensive medical issues, I required many operations, which led to me being hospitalized for the first twenty-three months of my life.

It was due to the extensive medical bills and surgeries that I had required, that I was nicknamed the million-dollar baby, and I became the poster child for BC CHILDREN'S hospital and was featured on the Variety Club Telethon.

Early on, the Ministry of Social Services, a department designed to protect children, became involved with my parents, because they had received a report from the hospital that they were concerned that my parents did not have the skills equipped to look after me. As I had a tracheotomy in my esophagus so I could breathe you had to be specially trained to deal with trach changes, and the mucus had to constantly be suctioned. I had other medical problems as well which would require massive medical supervision.

Although I was born with an extensive list of medical issues, I was still my parents' baby. The medical concerns, created a huge controversy over my care and what environment I should be raised. Knowing my parents did not have the education or training to deal with my health ailments, I was placed in government care immediately upon being discharged just a month shy of my second birthday as I spent the first 23 months from hospital. My parents had never had the opportunity, to look after me. They were never provided the chance to succeed or fail. They were never provided the resources to deal with my medical ailments either. The medical staff then contacted the Ministry and made a formal complaint.

Ministry of Social Services veteran social worker Jessica Tolson, received my file in the latter part of 1974. Tolson, a middle-aged woman with grey hair was a veteran in the child protection field. Throughout the years of working as a child protection social worker for the Ministry of Social Services in British Columbia, she had seen many horrifying cases, and had dealt with just about everything.

Ms. Tolson sat at her desk reviewing my case. Thinking to her that I was from a family that was drug addicted or young. It seemed to her that these days that's all she was getting was the mothers who were doing drugs while pregnant, or teenage parents who knew nothing about being parents as they were just children themselves. As she read the file on me, she began to realize that this was an entirely different case.

According to the file, Ms. Tolson read that I was born at 26 weeks gestation at one pound thirteen ounces. My parents were 24 and 36. They already had my sister who was two, and there was a history of domestic violence, alcoholism, and instability.

Primary concerns were that I had severe medical problems, such as an esophageal atresia without a fistula (in non-technical language a narrowing in my throat, which made it difficult to eat food, like other children my age). Reading further in my file Mrs. Tolson found that my mom visited very infrequently over the previous twenty-three months. In fact, my family very rarely came and visited me. Upon discharge, I would require tube feeding and extensive medical care as I could not walk without a walker and needed substantial assistance for daily living, more than usual for a child of my age of almost two. It was felt by hospital staff that I should be placed in a home where the caregivers had a medical background. This was so that my medical needs would not be neglected.

Jessica Tolson picked up the phone that sat on her desk and dialed my parent's number. The phone rang and just as Jessica was to hang up, a woman answered "Hello".

Jessica Tolson replied into the phone's handset "Hi may I speak to Jasmine or Hunter; this is Jessica Tolson from the Department of Social Services & Housing calling the woman on the other end of the phone identified herself as Jasmine. Mrs. Tolson continued to tell my mom that she was assigned to my case. My mother was told that there were concerns that if I were to be discharged from the hospital that there was some issues as to whether or not they could adequately provide for my needs, due to the over abundant medical care that I would require. It was at this time that my mother and father were informed that the Department of Social Services had apprehended me and would be placing me in a specialized foster home ensuring that I would get the medical care I required.

According to the Child, Family and Community Services Act in the Province of British Columbia Canada, Social Workers have the ability to remove a child whom they feel may be at risk of neglect or harm, or when they believe a child may be at risk of physical, emotional or sexual abuse, should they stay residing in their home environment. In this particular case, the removal was because I required extensive medical care, which it was felt that my parents could not provide me, due to their lack of medical knowledge.

Normal procedure when a Social Worker apprehends a child (takes the child into their custody, places their child in a foster home) a presentation hearing is made in a courtroom by a judge. In this particular case, my parents agreed to place me into the Department of Social Services care, because they did not know any better and they were informed that they would not place me for adoption without informing them of this. Shortly after my parents entered into a verbal agreement to place me in the Government's care, they moved to Edmonton Alberta, so that my father could find gainful employment. The Department of Social Services in British Columbia ceased to send my parents reports or documents pertaining to my care as they had agreed to, according to letters that were found in my file later. In August of 1976, the Department of Social Services placed a classified advertisement for a specialized foster home for me, as I was just about ready to be discharged for the first time from hospital.

On March 23, 1976, I was ready to be discharged from the hospital. My medical conditions were stable and hospital staff felt that I was becoming institutionalized from the hospital setting. The daunting task of locating a suitable home for me had been completed as Jessica Tolson decided to place me with forty-five year old Carol Jenkins, a registered nurse at the Vancouver Hospital. Carol Jenkins, already a recognized foster mother of 3 boys' ages five, twelve, and seventeen, and the biological mother of two daughters ages sixteen and nineteen.

Carol Jenkins had seen the advertisement in the local newspaper for the specialized foster home for me. Thinking to herself that she could look after my medical needs, she applied for the position. It appeared that Dianna's own parents had abandoned her at the hospital and fled to Alberta. On the outside Carol appeared to be a wonderful foster mother, caring, loving and very friendly, but inside the Jenkins household, it was completely different. This is something that I would not be able to talk about until much later in life, it was the beginning of a long journey through the foster care system. It was the start of being victimized by a system that was set up to protect me.

Chapter 2 "The Jenkins"

Carol Jenkins lived in a moderate five-bedroom home in the eastside of Vancouver, British Columbia Canada. The home itself was situated in a family friendly neighborhood, and there was a corner store on almost every city block. When you drive down the street, you can see the children playing in their yards and their parents nearby doing lawn maintenance.

Carol Jenkins was the foster parent of three boys Richard 17, David 12, Kenny 5, and the biological mother of two girls Helen 19, and Mary 16. The Jenkins household was quite chaotic, with such an age range in kids there is no wonder. Richard, who was the eldest of the boys was tall for his age, he had a very quiet demeanor and really did not socialize with anyone and hung out in his room as he had his own room in the basement. Richard had dark brown hair and brown eyes. Kenny and David shared a room and Helen and Mary did the same. Carol and I had our own rooms.

The layout of the house was rather simple, the kitchen was an open style with a door that led to the basement to where Richard slept and spent most of his time. Just off the kitchen were a unique living room with dark carpet and a step going down into it off the kitchen. Just off the living room, a staircase leads to the upstairs where the bedrooms were and the bathroom. Carol's cleanliness was something to be desired for, the home was extremely cluttered and dirty with dust throughout the house and looking around the house, you would think it had never been cleaned. This was documented in the Social Services file of Dianna Johnson.

Today was the day that I was to be placed so Carol ensured that the kids were all out doing their thing, so that she could have the undivided attention of Jessica Tolson, my social worker. She wanted to come across just right, after all she didn't want the warning bells to go off that she was only wanting me in her home for the extra money she would get for having me.

Heaven forbid one of the kids is there and the social worker catch her off guard and being mean to the kids.

It was half past noon, when Jessica Tolson arrived with me. There I was screaming bloody murder strapped in my car seat. A frazzled Jessica Tolson unstrapped me from the car seat, picked me up, and placed me on the ground. Carol, walked up to the car and said hi to me, and then looked at Jessica. You must be Jessica Tolson, I'm Carol nice to finally meet you. Carol extends her hand to shake Jessica's hand. Jessica grasped Carols hand quickly and introduced herself. She then walked over to me, taking a hold of my hand, and followed Carol into the house with me in tow. Jessica learned long ago, never get personal with the foster parents because then they think you can bend the rules for them. Her goal was to place me as fast as she could then hopefully start home before rush hour.

Inside, Carol showed Jessica Tolson the room that would belong to me; the room was bright with a single bed, and a bright yellow dresser in the corner. Jessica looked around the house and it seemed rather dirty to her, she figured perhaps with so many kids it was just hard to clean up after them. Thinking to herself Jessica decided to document it on her notepad just in case it ever came up later. Looking over at Carol she noticed that she was helping me take my coat and shoes off, and I was just staring at her, not making any noises or talking. Carol asked Jessica if I could talk. Jessica replied, "Yes I could talk but that I was not up to my age level of speech". Jessica assumed this was a very strange question to ask because she thought that Carol would know more about me than she let on after all she had visited me in the hospital according to her supervisor. Regardless, Jessica pulled out the paperwork that needed to be signed and explained to Carol, the formalities of the paperwork. Jessica continued to wonder if Carol was a suitable placement for this little girl.

The thought again Jessica kept pushing out of her mind after all, who all can keep a house clean with so many kids. Other than the messy house and the fact that Carol acted as if she had never met Dianna before, she seemed to be completely oblivious to the questions that were about to be asked. Although they were standard questions, they are necessary at the placement of the child. With Carol, already having three foster children placed with her you would think she would be used to the drill. After all the astronomical amount of paperwork the Ministry required, didn't change all that much in fact there was more to fill out than years earlier. As now, you needed a report for every little thing done on a child's file.

Jessica went on to explain the Ministry of Social Services & Housings job was to place children in foster homes, and that although the foster parent has the right to discipline and make minor decisions with respect to the daily care of the child, but ultimately if she had any major decisions a social worker would have to be contacted. Jessica further explained that foster parents are not allowed to use any sort of physical discipline to reprimand a child. Jessica read the following statement

as   part   of   a   formality:
"All foster parents must refrain from any physical
discipline such as spanking. Foster parents or solely
the day to day caregiver of the child, however all
decisions with respect to the child or emergency
medical consents must be signed for by the social
worker, or another person that is delegated by the
Ministry of Social Services and Housing. So I just need
your signature here informing that you understand
this." Carol nodded and signed the form.

Jessica then got up and put her papers back in
her briefcase, and said that she best be going. Carol
then asked when my belongings would be arriving, as
she had no money to buy me any. Jessica told Carol to
make a list that would be purchased the next day. Carol
replied are you sure, it takes forever for you to cut a
check. Jessica reassured Carol that there would
definitely be a check cut for her for any clothes or
other incidentals that I would require including any
medical supplies. Still thinking in her head that Carol
seemed to be very money motivated, she decided to
ask Carol why she had decided to take me into her
home. Well, replied Carol, I just love kids what can I
say, quickly going up to the door, I guess you best be
going it is about to be rush hour. Jessica looking at her
watch I guess I best be going if you ever need anything
just call me here is my card. Jessica handed her card to
Carol and left with Carol closing the door behind.

Looking at me, "I guess it's just you and me",
Carol stated. Just as she said this, all the other kids
come barreling in. Carol told the kids, that they all

needed to meet me. Dianna is new and will be staying with us awhile, and she is different then you. I need to tell you all the rules, first of all Dianna has to eat special food so in no way are any of you to give her food that is not blended. You are not to give her candy or anything else. Listening to Carol explain the rules , the kids said hi and went off in their own directions, while five year old Kenny lingered around staring at me, the new foster sister. Wondering if I was any fun to play with Kenny looked at me, and asked me if I liked blocks. I replied yes and smiled at him. Therefore, Kenny and I sat there playing blocks. Kenny became my companion, my friend, and when I was older, I truly thought we would catch up. I was wrong. I found a picture of Kenny and me when I was two and a half, and we were sitting on Santa Claus's knee. I liked Kenny.

Three years later···

As a five year old, I absolutely loved to explore my surroundings. Of course if you ever have had a five-year-old hanging around or if you have ever parented a five year old you would totally understand how they like to explore. I had been with the Jenkins now for about 3 years, and I became accustomed to living with Carol and the never-ending entourage of children she fostered over the years I resided with her. I loved to watch people well actually watching was an understatement, I loved to stick my middle finger up at old ladies and use bad words like "FUCK OFF", and watch as the little old lady would look at me in shock and then look at Carol Jenkins shaking their heads in disbelief. Imagine looking at cute little five-year-old girl that is dressed in a nice dress, and pigtails, dressed all pretty and looking like an angel but then they're holding their middle finger up. The scene is not only hilarious but also shocking all in the same time. That is what I did to people, I loved to shock people, not only as a child but still to this day. Not only did I have an issue with the words that came out of my mouth, but also I had a nasty habit of going up to people who were much larger than I was and pinching them in the line-ups at the grocery store. I just could not stop bothering people. Maybe it was because I was not taught proper etiquette, I truly do not know. For me it was fun.

Perhaps my shocking and annoying nature is what led to me being abused by Carol. I am not saying that it was my fault that I was abused, however, I do feel that even though I know it wasn't my fault I still feel that something about me caused the abuse to occur. I guess like most victims that are sexually abused, it is normal to blame yourself for what has happened. I just cannot understand why someone would want to have sex with a child, or even want to touch a child in such an inappropriate violating way. There is huge debate as to whether or not a five year old can remember sexual abuse that occurred to them as a child. Many research studies have shown that children whom are victims and are traumatized at a young age are less likely to remember it. However, there are many cases of where a child remembers things from when they are over the age of five. To this day, I do not know what started the abuse, if it was just her way of getting even with the fact that I was a horrible child or if it was because she was just sick and twisted. The abuse started shortly before my sixth birthday and really close to the time, I was to move in with my biological parents. I remember the first incident as if it was yesterday. I remember one night I woke up in the middle of the night and snuck downstairs and climbed up onto the countertop and snuck out the big jar of Kraft peanut butter. Opening the jar, I dug my little fingers into it and sucked it up into my mouth, just as I was finished the jar fell to the ground Carol ran down the stairs, curlers in her hair quickly putting her glasses on, started yelling what you are doing. She grabbed me roughly off the counter by the wrist, and yanked me all the way upstairs by my arm to the bathroom, where she turned on the shower. I was covered head to toe with peanut butter. Carol then placed me into the shower and held me under it. Shortly after she did, I realized it was an ice cold shower and not a warm one. Screaming and crying I scream NO! NO! It is cold. Carol just held me under the steady stream of ice-cold frigid water. After I was cleaned, up (to this day I have no idea how she could have cleaned the peanut butter off me with cold water, as it would be rather oily.) She placed me roughly in my room. After this incident, she consistently locked me in my room.

This was only the beginning of the abuse. It was well documented in my file that I was locked into a room for days at a time. If they did not lock me up, they would take me unnecessarily to the hospital for an admission so that they could get "RESPITE", (a break from me). I remember in a bedroom I was locked in it had large shelves that were made out of metal. I think it had make up and a bunch of other stuff on them, I got into it all, then I was in trouble, But I was five years old what five year old would not get into things when they are bored and they are explorers.

As a child, I had the common issue of wetting the bed. This is normal for children who for whatever reason cannot control their bladders while they are sleeping. I was a bed wetter, and because of this, I think it gave Carol Jenkins an excuse to abuse me. She would find that I had a wet bed and she would yank me from my bed and into the cold shower, it was never warm, it was always ice cold. I asked her why it had to be so cold; she would reply that to get rid of the urine it had to be cold. I have no idea if this explanation was true or not, but for a five year old what I was supposed to say. For days at a time, Carol would lock me in my bedroom, not just at night but also anytime during the day when she did not want to deal with me. For the most part Helen looked after me and Carol was off at the hospital working her nursing shift. Carol also used the hospital as a goal to have respite away from me. My health records showed that there were many hospitalizations that in reality I did not require being admitted.

I was not only physically and emotionally abused while living with Carol Jenkins, but I was also sexually abused for the first time while living in this foster home. Here I was five years old and having to go through the trauma of being violated in a way that you would never want anyone to go through. It began when Carol decided to show me a book about the female anatomy. I remember us sitting in her bedroom on her bed. She showed me a book that had pictures of the female body, it had a white and blue hard cover, and she then sat and started naming the parts of the female body. Now naming the parts of the female anatomy is not sexual abuse because children need to be able to name their body parts, however Carol took it much farther than just naming parts. She went on to tell me how to touch myself in certain ways, which would "tickle". She told me how to masturbate, and then took it even further by masturbating in front of me. After this sexual abuse, she encouraged me to masturbate, on a regular basis. Thinking back to it as an adult it absolutely appalls me that this woman was allowed to even have me in her home. When you are taught at such a young age this, you truly do not know if its normal or not, and you do believe it's okay because you don't know any different. For me I thought it was normal, and I guess that is why later on in life I continued to do it in front of people as I didn't think there was anything wrong with it.

One of the oldest boys also touched me inappropriately, but I don't remember exactly what he did or what the circumstances were. I remember it was Halloween and it happened in the basement and Richard, was the person who did it but that's about it. I think the reason I remember what Carol did was because of the fact it was more of a teaching with a book and physically showing me on herself. I was too young at the time to tell anyone about what was going on because I wasn't taught that what was going on was not okay. Although the abuse was well documented in my files, nothing was ever done. Which it seems to be a common occurrence when children whom are in the care of the provincial government are sexually abused. They are considered to "NOT BE BELIEVED" which I personally believe is BULLSHIT, because it is not the children's fault that they are placed into a home that has been abusive, it is the abusers fault for abusing the child. Since when is it okay for a foster parent to physically or sexually abuse a child in their care, since when is it okay for an adult to abuse a child at any time? If it was a child that was being abused by their parents let's just say social services are very quick to remove that child from the environment, even when there may be no evidence of such abuse, but it is the completely opposite for those who are children that are being abused in the Foster Care system. It's a double standard wouldn't you say.

Prior to writing this book I attempted to make contact with the Jenkins's family to interview them to allow them to tell their side of the story however, my request was denied.

According to my social services files, I made contact with the Jenkins when I was fifteen as well as older, I was trying to confront these people about what they did to me. Also according to my file the Jenkins family had accused me of harassing them, however I was only seeking answers about the abuse I had endured while residing with them.

Chapter 3 "The Reunion"

My mom and dad were ecstatic that their baby girl whom they gave birth to six years prior was finally coming home. Although my parents had only recently been allowed to visit me at the foster home, they felt that they could handle it. It was fantastic that my mom and dad would come and visit me, I remember when they told me they were my parents I was sitting on my dad's knee and I was doing a wool dot to dot, you know those cardboard pictures with holes that you put pieces of wool through. So my dad whispers to me "you know I am not your uncle, and I am your dad", and he points to my mom beside me and says that's your mom." So this is how I found out who my biological parents were.

It appeared that I didn't require the constant medical care which I used to require, although I still had medical issues, such as my trach and I couldn't eat solid food yet, I didn't require the extensive medical care that I had required prior. My parents now lived in a larger place, as they rented a main floor of a very large character house on Main Street in Vancouver, as Edmonton Alberta did not work out. My sister Laura-Lee was now almost 8, and very responsible. My sister was really looking forward to having a little sister and finally being able to play with me like she always dreamed of.

Laura-Lee and I shared a room. Laura-Lee was your typical eight-year-old but she was extremely gifted. She was smarter than most in her age group, after all she was reading from the age of two. Laura-Lee was the type of child that thought logically about everything. She was very head strong and smart. At first all seemed fine living with my biological family, however as the days grew into months there began to be problems. Due to the abuse that I had suffered in the Jenkins foster home, I still had a lot of anger built up, and I would have these huge temper tantrums where I would yell and scream for hours, and kick the walls and not listen to anyone. Part of the issue I suspect is my mom had not had the adequate amount of time to bond with me since I arrived in her care. It was like being pregnant for six months, going to the hospital delivering the baby, leaving the hospital and then 6 years later reuniting with that baby who no longer was a baby but a school age child. There was no bonding between us, and unfortunately the lack of the bond between mother and daughter really created havoc for years on my life.

Mom had struggles because my dad was continuing to drink, and when he was drunk he would beat her up. I never saw any of the abuse, I am aware that both my mother and sister have stated my father was abusive, however I truly have never seen it. Although, I have never seen it does not mean it happened or didn't happen, I just never witnessed it or I just don't recall it. What I do remember is my father always being away working and such. The main fight I remember between my mother and father was when my mother had made two large bologna sandwiches' she had sat down to eat them and the next thing I knew my mom and dad would fight and it would end up with her mother throwing the sandwich at the television set. Thinking back to these fights, I could not really understand why it occurred, however, as an adult it appears that my mother had food related issues and made everything surrounding food a fight.

The fighting was continuous between my parents; it would be focused on food, or about who was going to watch me, however domestic violence was not the only issue in the household. My mom's tolerance of my temper outbursts was less than to be desired for. My mom could not handle me, but in my opinion, she just did not want to handle me or treat me with respect, nurture me, or anything of the sort. The relationship between us was that of no bonding, lack of love and understanding, and one of complete strangers. It was like my mom didn't even know me but yet she had to raise this little monster as she called me. The relationship between Laura-Lee & I was total sibling rivalry. Laura-Lee knew she had a sister, and that sister was me, but she truly didn't understand why I was so angry and throwing so many temper tantrums.

The relationship between my sister and I could be classified as tense at times, but deep down we loved each other. Unfortunately, we never had the time to bond, after all I was in and out of foster care and we never got the opportunity to really get to know each other.

I truly do not really know my sister. I could not tell you what my sisters favorite color was, what type of music she likes, who her favorite actor or actors are, what her favorite movie is. I cannot tell you what her goals are in life, or what she loves the most. I cannot tell you whom she wants to be like. Nevertheless, what I can tell you is my sister is a beautiful person, inside and out. My sister is a loyal friend, honest and is a very caring person. If you were my sister's friend, she would stick up for you no matter what. My sister is a very caring woman who loves life to the fullest.

When writing this book my sister wanted me to withhold the publication, not to say she did not want me to write my book, because she too felt I had a story to tell and that it is a story that needs to be told. Initially she wanted me to hold off because she was concerned I would make my mom look bad. My sister means the world to me. She and I have been through a shitload of things together, mostly bad but some good as well. I love my sister, and regardless of the catfights, we had growing up, the fact is we love each other. We may not always tell each other this, and we may live countries apart, but we do love each other and are there for one another.

I respect my sister for her beliefs, her values and her as a person. I may not necessarily agree with everything she says, but she tends to hold substance when she talks. You know how you meet people who talk but just for the sake of talking, it does not seem to be important. Well my sister is not like that. When she talks, people listen because what she says is important and valid.

Going back to why there was so much upheaval in my house you see, I had a habit when I was throwing temper tantrums to scream at the top of my lungs and all the neighbors could hear was "OW stop hurting me", that hurts, and then of course the blood curdling screams from a child that sounded like they were being tortured. . This of course prompted Good Samaritan neighbors to call Social Services to have this checked out. Many visits from child protection services were due to these incidents. They would be checked out by a social worker only to be considered unfounded however there was abuse going on in the home but social services didn't get wind of it until I was about nine years old.

My mom was a very strict mother, and she expected everything her own way. Not only did she have to have her way all the time, she also consistently utilized health ailments, as issues as to why she could or could not do certain things. This would be reflected later on as well in my social services file. My sister and I attended school, together I was in Kindergarten as my birthday fell after December 31 so I started when I was six. Laura-Lee was in grade 2. At school I was not liked as I would steal lunches from the cloak room because I was very hungry, as my mom was at a loss of what to feed me as the doctors directions between Vancouver & Prince George had different opinions of what I can and could not eat. My father moved us to Prince George in 1981, so that he could continue to do long haul truck driving between Prince George and Vancouver. It was at this time that I entered grade 2 at Spruceland Elementary School.

It was at Spruceland Elementary that it became apparent that I was being neglected and abused at home. It began with me stealing lunches out of the cloakroom in the classroom because I was very hungry. Then when I wasn't able to do that it left me to dig through the garbage cans at the school. I remember at first sneaking into other kids back packs and taking out their sandwich's and quietly eating it. But then there came to a time where the teachers would catch on to me stealing the lunches from my classmates so I had to find an alternative way to eat, so I would look in the garbage cans, I was always very careful to pick items of food that were wrapped with a baggie so I wouldn't get sick. I remember one day I had a big score, someone had thrown out a peanut butter and jam sandwich into the dumpster inside the school, and it was wrapped in a sandwich baggie, it had no exposure to the air so I didn't have to worry about anything bad on it. I remember another time the school would have a Christmas Tree decorated in the hallway, and they would have boxes of wrapped food for the food bank and I would get into that too. I also remember climbing into a big dumpster and eating a piece of chocolate cake. Thinking back to it I am very surprised I never got sick. Life at home wasn't any better as I was almost nine, and I still couldn't eat like everyone else. I could eat more than what my mother would allow me too, but I still was not the same as everyone else my age.

Going through school, not being able to eat solid food because your mom won't give it to you was difficult. I had a really difficult time. My lunches were mostly a can of Ensure, that was about it. As I write this it's hard, because I think to myself do I sugar coat it and defend my mom for her actions, knowing she is alive and well and may one day read this, or should I tell the truth about how her actions affected me? I'm torn between the truth and deciding whether or not to tell how I feel about the whole situation. Knowing it is a story that has needed to be told for an extensive amount of time I chose to tell what happened.

The feelings of indifference and inadequacy among my peers in school created the lack of ability to make long lasting friends. After all what parent would allow their child to play with a child that eats out of the garbage cans. Obviously there would be substantial issues at home.

Just to give you an idea of the diet restrictions that my mother had me on was, blended everything. You are probably sitting there thinking to yourself okay she has medical issues. Have you ever tasted bread that is blended with tons of water? Or what about cold lumpy cream of wheat, it is absolutely disgusting, I wouldn't serve it to my dog let alone my child, to this day I cannot fathom why my mother didn't feed me infant formula or baby food. If I didn't eat what my mother served to me whether it be the cold cream of wheat, or blended bread, it went in the refrigerator until the next day or meal.

Let's just say I never ate because it was gross, I would throw it up because it was disgusting. The tension in the household became overwhelming for me. Here I was nine years old almost, and I was different, I was treated so inhumanely. I couldn't eat food like everyone else, I couldn't sneak food anymore because my mom would put dish soap all over the left over's on the dishes, (before she did this I would eat the crumbs as I was starving). As I wasn't allowed to eat, I was still forced to stand there and do the dishes with my sister. It was tough.

My mom was a big time baker, she baked everything you could think of, from homemade cinnamon buns, to bread, cakes and tarts, she baked it all, and I couldn't have any of it. To a child whose nine and has never had anything explained to her it was torture having to not only smell the wonderful delicious food but not being allowed to eat it.

It was at this time that I decided if my mom didn't want me fine I'd go find someone else who did and I did what any child would have done. I ran away from home at the age of nine. Where does a nine year old go? I went to our next door neighbors.

That's right I went up to the neighbors door and banged on it and a really nice old lady answered it and she was so nice and invited me in and offered me a cup of warm milk and supper. I was so excited, sat down, ate normal food, and drank the warm milk without any issues with my throat.

Guess I chewed it well. At the time I was with this little old lady, I didn't realize that she was our landlady and actually had rented our house to us. I remember when the telephone that was hanging on the wall in the kitchen rang, and the woman answered it and then everything happened so fast, all of a sudden, my parents were at the door and picked me up.

They took me home, and it was at this time my father gave me a spanking that I would never forget. I truly believe I scared my dad that day. I think he was worried that something bad had happened to me because they had no idea where I was, and they most definitely knew that I did not have any friends.

Upon my return, my mom forced me to drink three large glasses of water because this was her way of seeing if my esophagus was blocked, because if the water could not go down than I would throw up, so then she would know to take me to the hospital. I think my neighbor thought she heard my parents beating me because it was at this time social services were called and they decided to apprehend me.

The grounds this time according to the social services file for apprehension were neglect, and physical abuse. According to my records I informed the social workers that my mom would dunk my head in the dish water and try to drown me and that my dad saved me. I also told how my mother would hit me over the head with everything from spoons, to knitting needles. I recalled how my mother didn't like the fact that I would pee the bed and that my own mother made me wash out my bed sheets in the basement with ammonia. I remember screaming, yelling, and not wanting to wash the sheets out.

My mother made me do it anyways. Living with my mom was a nightmare. I know that my mother, only used the skills she knew how to at the time, and made her share of mistakes, as many parents do.

I do not hold her for blame for anything that happened in my past, because I am sure I was not an easy child to deal with, as well as we have made amends with what happened and I have found peace with this. I have not forgotten what happened, living with my mom, however I have forgiven her and I love her.

My mother as a way to cope with me decided to lock me in my room as well with only a pail to go to the bathroom in. At first I couldn't understand why my mother would do this as well considering it was a common occurrence when I lived in the Jenkins household. Unfortunately, it also occurred with my mom. I was painted a very nasty picture of my mother, from someone whom knew me growing up who now is an adult themselves. They witnessed firsthand the treatment I received at the hands of my mother. While writing this book, I discussed these incidents with both my mother and my sister.

My mother apologized for her part in what happened to me, and also informed me that I was a monster child, and that if she could go back in time she would do things differently. My mom went on to say that she was not provided any resources on how to deal with the behavior that I was exhibiting. She also blames the fact that I was an animal when she got me, I would pinch scratch, hit, bite, I had diarrhea constantly and that she was feeding me but it would come out both ends. All of these were the reasons my mother gave me for what occurred. My mother and I sat down and discussed this shortly prior to the release of "Daughter's Choice".

Although I may not necessarily agree with her reasoning behind the abuse I endured at her hands, I forgive her for what happened. I have to forgive her for what happened, because in my opinion she is a very self centered woman whom craves attention for herself. She always had to act like she was sick to get people to feel sorry for her. However, thus being said my mother is my mother. She is family as my sister once said; Family sticks together no matter what. Unfortunately, in this particular case my sister is wrong. I cannot stand by a woman who claims to be my mother only to be emotionally hurt by her even in adulthood.

When I received a call from my sister Laura-Lee asking me to not release my book until after our mother passes (although she is nowhere near her deathbed) I debated about it. People want many things I wanted a family who loved me , accepted me for who I am, I wanted a mother who LOVED me, who treated me equally to her other child, and I never received that. Why should I spare my mother the embarrassment of the truth that occurred with me growing up?

This book is not about how bad my mother was to me. It is about how I went through hell and back and grew up in over twenty-three different homes, only to come out on top. It is a story of hard work, healing and perseverance. During the day my mother would lock me in the room 24/7 and the little girl (my friend as an adult now) always wondered why I was not allowed out to play. My mother said that I was a bad kid. And then there was my sister who didn't have to do anything and was treated like gold I, at this point couldn't understand why my mother had even wanted me back in the first place if this was the way she was going to treat me. All I wanted was a mother who loved me. I can recall one incident where my mom drove me to Fort George Park, and just dropped me off and she told me that I would never see her again. I remember clutching the passenger side mirror of the car, screaming at my mother to stop that I was scared that I didn't want her to leave me. I was terrified, she didn't end up leaving me there but she could have. To this day this is an incident that my mother denies ever happening. However, I remember this as if it were yesterday.

I know I wasn't perfect, but I was also a child. I didn't deserve to have what happened to me happen. I remember my mother would pound on my chest like a percussion claiming it was physiotherapy that she had to do it. I hated this because she hit me so hard that I would get bruises on my chest and my back. I remember one time I got so mad we had a storm glass window door, and I punched it and it broke. I finally ended up running away.

It was after I had run away, the social workers finally realized that I was being abused, so they kept me in their care, and placed me in a foster home that was situated out on a farm. Finally thinking that I would be safe, I was in for an even greater surprise. I would soon realize that although I was once again being placed into a system which was set up to protect me I would not be protected.

The Social Workers did not have any evidence that I required protection from my mother according to my social services file that is. It came to be known that a social worker, my child psychiatrist, another Doctor, a pediatric nurse, all had a meeting about me.

The object of the conference was to see if the Ministry of Social Services, had enough evidence to stand up in court and say that my mother was an unfit mother.

The complaints that the Ministry were trying to deal with were the fact that they believed my mother was starving me, and that my mother suffered from Munchausen's Biproxy Disorder. At no time have I ever received confirmation that my mother had this disorder, and I have seen that in the medical records for me early on it has no reference to any of this. I do not believe my mother ever made me sick. I do believe she was torn between the medical professionals in Vancouver BC whom instructed her on a particular diet, and the other medical personnel in Prince George who stated the opposite. The sole purpose of the case conference was to devise a plan, which my mother would go along with, in order to gain evidence against her that she was abusing me.

In order to implement this plan I had to be placed in a foster home on a Farm for several weeks in order to provide the Ministry time to establish evidence that would hold up in court solidly.

The following is a paraphrased case conference report from this meeting that the Ministry of Social Services had with respect to their plan for me and their plan to trick my mother.

Present at the case conference were Dr. June Frye (child psychiatrist, Dr. Terry Meadows, Joyce B, Noreen B. Social Worker, Pat Storey, Michelle Demers (social worker), and Patricia Burleigh R.N.

The conversation begins with everyone introducing themselves, and then Dr. June Frye states that she sees me twice, prior to the meeting they were having, and that the first time she saw me, my mother had an appointment with Dr. Russ Frye, at the same time. When Dr. June Frye saw me I was very scared to go into the playroom because my parents wouldn't allow me to.

I guess from the meeting my mother felt that if I was playing that it is fun and not psychotherapy, and they felt this wouldn't help me. Dr. Frye goes on to state how she explained how it helped me, and she even explained that she spoke to a child psychiatrist in Vancouver who also had reiterated to my mother that it would help me.

Dr. June Frye, carries on and tells the group in the meeting how I was very frightened to play, and that she would reassure me and speak to my mom about it. She stated that she tells my mom after she saw Dr. Russ Frye, and that my mother replied "Fine ! Yes, I know I know, I have been told this alright for her to come in here." (the playroom). During the course of the interview I had with Dr. Frye, I was hungry so Dr. Frye gave me a cookie, which her secretary May had made. Dr. Frye goes on to state how nothing is said by my mom until after the first time and when the second appointment came around my mom called Dr. Frye. When my mom called she was quite paranoid according to Dr. Frye, and continued to tell her that I couldn't go back to the psychiatric appointments anymore, and that the cookies were hurting me. , that it was dangerous for me, and that the full diet that I had been on in the Hospital had also been dangerous for me. According to the Dr. June Fry my mother admitted to being anxious and upset, but she agreed for me to continue to see the psychiatrist.

Then apparently about a week later, my mother called the secretary and informed her that I would not be returning.

The social worker Noreen then discusses how she thinks she knew my family and then all of a sudden she states it's very difficult to tell whether my behavior and physical problems are emotionally based, and how much they are not. She goes on to discuss how it's obvious I have some emotional problems but she is not sure as to whether or not my mom is the cause of all my problems. They claimed that while I was hospitalized I did not have diarrhea, or vomiting to the extent, my mother claimed I had.

The social workers and doctors then go on to discuss how they are going to trick my mother into allowing me to stay out on the farm at Joyce B's, so that they can decide whether or not my issues with diarrhea and vomiting are accurate or if it is my mother's doing. They also wanted to know if it was true that I would sneak food. They continued to discuss as to how they felt my mother was deliberately making me be sick by forcing me to drink tons of water, they also went on to accuse my mother of doing all of this for attention for herself and claimed she had Munchausen's by proxy. . Although there was never any evidence to back this up in any of my case files, I can tell you that I remember on one occasion of going to Dr. June Frye's office, and eating the oatmeal cookies that her secretary had made, and I can most certainly say that I did get it blocked because I didn't chew it properly, I remember this as if it was yesterday.

I also believe at the time my mother truly didn't know what to do and she was caught in a war between hospitals and doctors between a small hick town and a big city. The conversation that took place at this meeting was a meeting to personally attack my mother, and try to use it as a way to gain evidence for a court case that my mother had abused me some way.

Yes my mother actions ended up starving me, however, I do not believe that she intended to do it. I truly believe she felt that she was protecting me. I truly do not believe that she did this on purpose. I remember wanting to eat, I would be stuck doing dinner dishes with my sister and I would see little pieces of burnt chicken on the pan I would sneak it quietly, so that my mom didn't know. Eventually my mother caught on and started spraying dish soap all over it and telling me it was poisonous, she also put rat poison on some stuff and told me that if I ate it I would die.

It was really bad. My mother was an avid baker and a damn good one and I had to sit and smell the lovely aroma's of my mom's baking but I wasn't allowed to eat any of it.

It was tough, so with all of this going on, the social workers had the meeting to check out to see if my mom was in fact starving me. One of the primary issues that the social worker, and doctors had was that they had to convince my mother to let me go to the farm. That was tough.

When I read of how the Ministry of Social Services planned to set my mother up I was completely appalled. Not once in my file did I see them offer her resources to deal with me.

Granted, she could have asked for help as well. It certainly does not justify the abuse I endured, however, parenting does not come with a handbook, how many babies do you know of are born with an instruction manual when they come out of you, In a vaginal delivery they most certainly don't neither do they in a Caesarian Section.

How does a parent go from giving birth to a child who you are told by doctors and nurses to not get close to because your child may die at any time to bonding with that child.

I believe this is the issue that my mom faced. She was scared to bond with me, because doctors and nurses consistently told her that I was going to die due to the extensive medical issues I had. So mentally she detached herself from me. Then when I lived and was out of the woods medically speaking, she had a hard time believing this and was still too scared to attach herself to me.

In no way do I believe that what my mother did to me was okay, however I can understand the explanation that I was given to me for what happened.

I do however, feel that the Ministry of Social Services should have provided my mother the resources such as counseling to help her deal with the emotional issues that surrounded my return to her home. I believe she was traumatized with my birth and what had happened, and she was so scared to have me.

Chapter 4 "Farm Life"

If you grew up in a city than you understand the hustle and bustle of people and traffic, however when you live on a farm, what we are used to as city folk I think is taken for granted. The social workers came to pick me up and take me to my new foster home. Unfortunately this home was not in the city, it was in fact just outside the Prince George city limits and it was situated on a farm.

Quite a culture shock for little old me, although I was nine years old now I was quite terrified to go and live on a farm. I wasn't used to farm animals and was scared of anything that had four legs. The house was situation by the Buckhorn Elementary School, just outside of Prince George city limits. My new family consisted of Rick & Joyce Thompson, Tannis Thompson, Marvin Thompson, Shane, and then myself. Rick was the stay at home foster dad, Joyce was a registered nurse and was the foster mother, and Tannis was their daughter and Marvin well he was their adopted son, and then there was Shane who just happened to be another foster kid just like me.

The typical daily routine with the Thompson's consisted of an early wake up at 6:00 am to go and feed the horses, collect the eggs from the chicken coop and of course, feed the darn critters. Then we had the task of feeding slop to the pigs, and other tedious farm chores like cleaning up after the horses, and pitching hay, all these chores of course were expected to be completed prior to breakfast, and heading to school. I was nine can you imagine, having to do farm chores, well actually being thrust into this lifestyle when you are raised in the city, I know I couldn't imagine it but here I was thrust into it.

Shortly after moving in with the Thompson's, I started dealing with some issues, that well let's just say no one should have ever had to deal with. Marvin, one of the other foster kids, who was like 16, or so had some huge issues, with wanting to touch girls where they shouldn't. It was during this time that I was sexually abused again in the care of the government. I made reports after reports about this and it took forever for the social worker to come and talk about it.

It all began when Marvin, my foster brother at the time, caught me up in the loft, and pulled me into one of the empty rooms. He told me that he had this wonderful game we could play called Flush the Toilet. Not knowing how to play the game, but wanting to play with someone, I played along with him. How you play this game is a boy will lay down on his back and put his feet up in the air while the other person sits on the feet of the person laying on their back, then the player that is sitting on the feet pushes the person's arm and then they say FLUSH and then at the same time the person with their feet in the air pushes the other person through the air and they go flying. So not only was this game dangerous, Marvin took it farther and decided to use this as an opportunity to sexually molest me. He tied me up and started touching me. This wasn't the only sexual abuse that occurred at this home. It was in this home which Rick Thompson sexually abused me, he forced me to have oral sex with him, as well as he always had me sitting on his lap so he could rub his leg into my vaginal area.

I complained to the Ministry of Social Services about this situation, and they sent my social worker Noreen to come out and interview me. Of course the foster parents decided to twist what was happening, and stated that I was showing signs of being sexually abused, and that it was probably because of my parents. This of course is completely false I was never sexually abused by my parents. During Noreen's visit, she created a transcript of the audio of what took place during the interview with me regarding the sexual abuse. Here is an excerpt with respect to the transcript, as it is quite lengthily to read and difficult to understand. The conversation took place in the living room of the farm house, and Rick, Joyce, the social worker Noreen and myself were present. I was nine years of age at the time, and Noreen had brought over four dolls that were anatomically correct, meaning they had the correct body parts on them. We were sitting down and playing with the dolls, and this is what verbally transpired.

SOCIAL WORKER: Do you remember the other day when you were here with Lillianne, in the living room?

DIANNA: Yeah.
SOCIAL WORKER: And you had your Minnie.
DIANNA: Yeah.

SOCIAL WORKER: Yeah, and you were playing in the living room. What happened then, do you remember?

D: Uh-

SOCIAL WORKER: What did she say to you?

DIANNA: Who?

SOCIAL WORKER: Lillianne.

DIANNA: I forget

RICK: Remember it was the day after you were at Mr.Bennett's house—

DIANNA: Yeah I knew that.

RICK: And Lillianne asked you if you knew what a lesbian was?

DIANNA: Oh, yeah yeah.

SOCIAL WORKER: And then what happened?

DIANNA: I told her.

SOCIAL WORKER: Well what do you think it is?

DIANNA Oh, I think

RICK: Why?

DIANNA: You know, big tummies.

SOCIAL WORKERS: You think it's what

DIANNA: A person that makes babies.

SOCIAL WORKER: A Lesbian is?

DIANNA: Yes.

SOCIAL WORKER: I didn't think that's what you said that day.

DIANNA: Well, isn't that– What'd I say?

RICK: Well, do you remember how you showed me how you rubbed yourself? Well, not me but you showed everybody in the living room.

DIANNA: What do you mean?

RICK: Remember? You stood up there and rubbed yourself and you sat on your teddy?

SOCIAL WORKER: Then you were rubbing yourself?

DIANNA: Look at me?

SOCIAL   WORKER: With   your   hand?

DIANNA: I know

RICK: Remember how you stood up and showed Lillianne how you rubbed yourself?

DIANNA: No, this was it.

RICK: Well, you did that to the teddy bear.

DIANNA: Yeah

RICK: And remember Lillianne said , "Stop get off the bear". Then you jumped off the bear and do you remember how you rubbed yourself?

DIANNA: Oh, yeah I don't. I think I just did this. Well I don't even want to tell you it's embarrassing. This is what I did. Like that

RICK: Yeah except you stood up. That's probably because Lillianne was pulling you off the teddy bear.

DIANNA: what

RICK: You were standing up probably because Lillianne was yanking you off the top of the bear.

SOCIAL WORKER: See, these dolls have all the parts and you can do them without having to do it to yourself see. So you can – so this is Dianna, Okay?

DIANNA: Yeah.

SOCIAL WORKER: So we'll have her available here so you can do it to this doll okay?

DIANNA: What do you mean?

RICK: Then you won't be embarrassed.

SOCIAL WORKER: see, you don't have to do it to yourself you won't be embarrassed.

DIANNA: What do you mean do that to me?

SOCIAL WORKER: No, I'll just take her nightie off so you can ---
DIANNA: I don't know what you are talking about.
SOCIAL WORKER: Well, just pretend this is you
DIANNA: Okay
SOCIAL WORKER, well just pretend like this is you and then you can have the doll do it and you don't have to do it.
DIANNA: Yeah, but I can't do it, that way I don't think.
JOYCE: That's   not   embarrassing   is   it?
Dianna: It's dumb
RICK: When you were playing like that time, was Minnie a boy or a girl?
DIANNA: Boy
RICK: It was a boy
SOCIAL WORKER: Do you want Dianna here?
DIANNA: No, I'll use Minnie and him cause he has
SOCIAL WORKER: Yeah but Dianna's a girl
DIANNA: Yeah, but I'm using this is what people do when they hump/ I mean you know what I mean eh.
RICK: Uh HUH
DIANNA: I know it's
RICK: It's not a bad word.
SOCIAL WORKER: If you - If you lay Dad down that might be easier,
DIANNA: Like How?
SOCIAL WORKER: Or if you lay Dianna down---
DIANNA: ON top?
SOCIAL WORKER: -- It might be yes or whatever.
DIANNA: I wonder how people Oh, I see. I know how you two got kids.
RICK: HOW

DIANNA: Same thing as I'm doing right now.

RICK: Uh-huh, that's how people reproduce.

DIANNA: I wonder how you do it. Well this is what people—

SOCIAL WORKER: So what do you call that?

JOYCE: Do you want to try with those?

DIANNA: Yeah she's bigger don't cross your legs dear I just want to have your baby. I'm going to pretend she wasn't born yet okay? There. Then you're at the hospital and here's the baby. And you're in the hospital too and this is the hospital now.

JOYCE: And she has to come in pregnant here.

DIANNA: How? Oh, I see Oh

SOCIAL WORKER: My goodness, wasn't Dianna born with a lot of hair?

JOYCE: Oh, dear I think I'm going to have my baby soon.

DIANNA: Okay OKAY , here Just a second. Get up on this bed. Okay where's your father?

JOYCE: He's out filling out papers for me

DIANNA: Okay, somebody else has to be here. They have to.   She has to take big big breaths. (Unintelligible) come out. Get it out. It's coming out do it again. Here is the hair.

SOCIAL WORKER: Lots of hair.

DIANNA: Here's your baby.

Joyce: Oh my baby isn't she gorgeous. Isn't she nice.

DIANNA: Lots of hair eh?

Baby is born Dianna gets her something to eat and everybody tries to decide on baby's name.

DIANNA: I wonder what the tape sounds like now can I listen to it?
SOCIAL WORKER: Not until we are finished.

RICK: Do you know how a girl plays with herself How does a boy do it?
DIANNA: I don't know. I think this is how I'm not sure. You just do this (plays with the doll)
RICK: How did you know that?
DIANNA: I don't know I just took a guess am I right?

During the rest of the transcript it went on to where the adults were trying to convince me that my mother had sexually abused me and this was absolutely false. They kept suggesting me to do this that and everything else with these dolls, I was a nine year old child in a room of three adults, which I personally felt very intimidated, into doing what they told me to do. While reading the transcript for this book I felt that the people that ran this should have been held accountable for their actions.

The whole purpose of putting me with the Thompson's on their farm was to establish as to what foods I had ever eaten, and to see whether or not I had been sexually abused. During the interview with the dolls, the social worker and the foster parents tried to claim that my mother had taught me how to touch myself etc. But this of course I venomously denied. As the real person that had taught me to touch myself was Carol Jenkins in my first foster home.

The interrogation techniques that the Social Worker, and the foster parents utilized while getting me to play with the anatomically correct dolls would possible be considered abuse all on its own. Since when is it ok to steer a child into the direction of positioning dolls on top of each other, and role play sexual acts. Although, they had asked me, I specifically stated I did not know what they meant, or what I was supposed to do with the dolls . Assuming that this signifies, that I had never been exposed to those types of sexual act previously, and the Adults had to teach me what to do with the dolls and also tell me what the act was called. If this isn't sexual abuse than what is it?

Living at the Thompson's was tough, each day because of the rural area we lived in we had to get on a school bus to attend school. I myself attended Buckhorn Elementary School.

Buckhorn Elementary School was located in Prince George British Columbia, and it first opened in 1931 with only two class rooms. Initially Buckhorn was opened due to families who preferred rural living arrangements were found to be attendance from all walks of life and income according to the school's website. In 1976, the school received a gymnasium and a library, and further additions were done in the sixties to allow more classrooms to be added.

As the school bell rang each day we had to race outside and we were loaded onto the big yellow school buses. I hated taking the bus because I was constantly picked on. Unfortunately this was the only transportation I had because Rick & Joyce refused to drive me to school. I remember my bike that my dad bought me, they let me take it out to the farm. I forgot to move it and Rick ran over it with his vehicle. This is how horrible it was at the Thompson's. The sad part of it was they were part of this huge plan to nail my mother and accuse her of abusing me although I was being abused there at the farm much worse than I was every abused at home.

I hated living with the Thompson's I wanted to go home. My mom and dad were not sexually abusing me, like the social workers were trying to find out during the interview with the dolls . My mother may not have always made the proper choice as to what to feed me due to the medical controversy between doctors in Vancouver and doctors in Prince George. This foster home was a nightmare, I was being sexually abused by Marvin, and that is the reason I started having issues there and started exhibiting sexual behavior in front of people. I believe my mom would probably say otherwise, considering she seems to believe that I had huge issues with sexual stuff. I found a letter in my files from when I was nine my mom had written in her own handwriting that I was not allowed to wear makeup because I would use it to get guys attention. I was nine, how many nine year olds knows about guys? Just curious I know most nine year olds don't even think about that. I had decided that I would do everything in my power to get kicked out of the Thompson's so that I wouldn't have to deal with the sexual abuse, and living in fear of the older boys. During this placement too Rick made me perform oral sex on him, again another form of sexual abuse. My mission was to get kicked out. It all began with me inviting the neighbor over I had been snooping through Rick and Joyce's room and found a big container of boxes of matches. So I stole several books of them and lit them lining them up on the window sill. Luckily for me I didn't light the house on fire, but I remember when they caught me, Rick got angry, Joyce was working a graveyard shift at the hospital, and I had to sleep with my stuffed mouse named Minnie, in the living room. The next day I was sent back to my parents, shortly after this I ended up having to have a major surgery because my throat had bulged out to the point where I couldn't eat anymore. My mother claimed that it was because of my apprehension and me being given to the Thompson's and how they allowed me to eat everything under the son, I can't find any documents to support this theory nor anything to claim it is not true either, given this I don't know who frankly to believe.

Chapter 5 "Yew Street"

My time at the Thompson's house became short lived. Thank God for that considering the tons of abuse that I had to deal with from both the foster parents and of course Marvin. I had been booted out officially the next day after I got caught playing with matches. I had lit up a bunch of plastic bottles with matches. Stupid me I didn't know that plastic melted. I guess I didn't really think about my actions. It seems very common even later in life I didn't really think about my actions. I scared the Thompson's, and what I didn't know was the Thompson's had lost their home to a fire a year or so before my arrival. So I guess my playing with fire sure didn't make Rick a happy camper. He was a jerk anyways and should never have been a foster parent to begin with again this was my opinion. I didn't like Rick. I hated him with a passion. I don't know if it was just because of the abuse he got away with or because he wasn't my father, and I had to deal with being taken away from my family and I was nine. Here I was nine and I had already been in several different homes. I was allowed to move back home for a couple years until I was eleven at which time my mother couldn't handle my behavior and she placed be in government care. Due to still being under the Department of Social Service's Care I was placed this time in a group home, rather than a foster home. This was because no family would take me. I was eleven and just entering grade seven. I was placed in a group home in the downtown core of Prince George called Yew Street Group Home, this home was part of the Prince George Receiving Home Society. The house was a 10 bed facility which had a boys wing and a girls wing. The children that lived in the group home ranged in age from eleven to nineteen years of age.

The house itself appeared from the outside, to look like an ordinary home that any family would live in. It was built in an L shape and was one story. Inside the building itself when you first walk in to the left you'll find a small office, then directly beside that you'll see another room with a glass door, and books with a small table and some chairs, this was the library. Then to your right is the television room where you would find a television that was behind a locked cabinet and a large overstuffed brown couch, and a recliner chair. To the right is an open concept kitchen and dining room. You'll find the long banquet style brown tables with chairs that don't move. The wall décor was pretty institutionalized off white walls with the odd picture of flowers. Just off of the dining room, you will see the largest kitchen ever that had commercial appliances. They had the stainless steel grill, the dish sprayer and sanitizing machine you would find in a restaurant. It looked like you stepped into a kitchen that you would find in a commercial setting not a house. Then of course you see the 4 big refrigerators and a huge walk in freezer.

Group Homes are a very unique living environment as it is run by staff members whom circulate on a shift work basis. Unlike the foster home which is more of a residential setting, a group home is more institutionalized. The purpose for opening group homes was to provide a temporary placement of youth that are in need of immediate housing, which can also handle high numbers of individuals in one accommodation.

While I was living in Yew Street group home, I would run away a lot. There was this one boy named Willie L. he was the same ages as me and he was tiny. There used to be a field close to where the home was situated so we would run through there. Now there is a church built on it, but at the time it was just a vacant lot, where kids would start little brush fires, and hide out with their friends. Willie and I would walk around downtown and just talk. Truly he was a friend, we were always on the lookout for the police of course because when you're in government care, the police are called and they pick you up and take you back to the foster home or group home depending which one you live in. I remember this one night that Willie and I ran away, we just did it because we wanted to, I remember I had these stupid white runners, with Velcro that you put on they were kind of like slippers. Anyways, we took off and walked around town for several hours. We always stayed close to the group home because quite frankly we didn't really want to run we were just testing their boundaries. Anyways we went back to the house. I remember seeing a police officer pull up to the house, I assume they were looking for Willie and I. I walked up and the police officer who asked me if I knew where Willie was, I said that I would go get him, I left with no intentions of getting him. I waited about twenty minutes or so before returning to the group home, and no and behold the police officer was still there. I was on probation at the time as well and I did not want to be arrested for breach of probation, as part of my probation I was to follow the rules at the group home and not runaway. I walked in and I didn't have my shoes on as I had already taken them off and sat down on the overstuffed chair in the living room. The police officer walked up to me and I knew I was going to be arrested, and there was no way I was going to allow this to happen without a fight. The police officer informed me that he was arresting me for breach of probation and that I needed to get my shoes on. Now picture this, a little petite girl that weighs perhaps 90 lbs, soaking wet and a police officer who is six four two hundred pounds, the bigger person is going to win. I remember reaching over putting my one shoe on then I was going to take off, or I threw it at the cop, I don't really remember what order. The cop said that I was going to go with him either the easy way or the hard way. Unfortunately for me I chose the hard way. Stupid me I decided to freak out, and start kicking this cop in his private area. Big mistake. He grabbed me so quickly and shoved me into the chair and handcuffed me behind my back and to hell with my shoes he yarded me by the handcuffs, outside to his car where he placed me in the backseat. I started kicking at the windows trying to break them. Eventually I calmed down and I was held in holding cells until the next day at which time I was released by the judge in court. I was very fortunate that the police officer did not charge me with assault. I was then returned back to the Yew Street group home and I wasn't there long before my grandma died. My mom and sister came to the group home and told me that Grandma had died of cancer. I was devastated. My grandmother, who was my mother's mom, was what kept my family together. It was shortly after my Grandma died that my own mother stopped being my mom and the distance totally grew between us, at least this is how I felt.

I wasn't a bad kid I just didn't like living in the foster care system. All I wanted was a family to call my own. I wanted to be accepted, I wanted to have unconditional love, and I wanted people to care about me not because they were paid to care about me or because it was their job to but because they really did care about me. Living at Yew Street Group Home was very difficult for me mainly because it was the first group home setting I had ever lived in and also because the majority of the other kids were much older than myself. I remember there was one kid named Jeremy G. He had red hair and very geeky looking. Jeremy had this habit of molesting the girls that he was in care with. And again nothing was done. Shortly after my grandmother passed, I moved back in mom and dad and my sister. Only to find out that my mother and father were getting a divorce and that my mother had a new boyfriend soon to be husband.

Chapter 6 "Last Time Home"

It was the beginning of September, I was just entering grade seven at Ron Brent Elementary when I was told by my social worker that I would be returning home to my family. However there would be a big change at home, my father would not be living with my mom as they were separating. My mother, my sister and myself were going to be living in an apartment just the three of us.

Here once again I felt rejected. Now my dad wasn't around to protect me if my mom decided to lose control of her anger and hurt me. I loved my dad so much and just wanted a relationship with him. My mother felt something differently about my reasons for wanting a relationship with my father. As far as I am concerned it was her issues not mine. It was during this time being back with my mom and sister only I realized that my mother viewed me as someone who was not her daughter. She consistently picked my sister as her favorite. My sister was allowed to do everything. She was allowed to watch "Days of Our Lives", at lunch time but I wasn't had to sit my back to the television set and heaven forbid I ever watch it or even look at the screen. I had to sit for hours on end doing long division, even though I didn't know how to do it. If I talked back to my mom she had these bowls of hard lentil beans and she would make me kneel in them, and I had to stay there it left impressions on my knees. I would get bored and pick my nose and wipe it on the wall.

My mom hated me. I was the daughter she had but never really wanted. I was my mother's excuse for everything that went wrong in her life. I was responsible for my dad leaving; after all I caused them too much stress. I was also an avenue for my mother to get attention for herself.

Heaven forbid my mother actually be a mother and treat me with respect, and dignity. My mom was my mom, and although I didn't like the way that she treated me so differently than my sister, she was still my mom and I loved her so much, more than the world would know. I couldn't do anything to change my mom. The way my mom would handle things is act like it always had to be someone else's fault, or she would constantly state that she was sick and she couldn't do this and couldn't do that because she had a headache or she was tired.

I remember many times how my mother used food as an issue with me. For starters, I did not like cream of wheat cereal. For whatever reason I just did not like this type of cereal. If I refused to eat it my mom would put it in the Refrigerator, and offer it to me at the next meal ice cold. She never offered to warm it up. It was cold and lumpy and I would throw up trying to eat it because it was disgusting.

Other things my mother would do is tease me with food, for example she would make a really nice sandwich or something and ask me if I wanted it then she would turn around and say sorry you can't eat it. I remember a couple incidents the most, I was about eight, I think and we were living in a big brown house on Ahbau Street in Prince George. My dad wasn't home for whatever reason I think he was working, and my mom had just done some canning. I got into her canning. Man was she upset when she found out. I was really hungry and I didn't' know what to do. My mother had bought this big red lunch kit that was made out of plastic, and all she would put in it was a can of Ensure.

My mom and a misconception as to what I could and couldn't eat. I like to think that it was just an oversight on her part but with everything that I remember and things that were stated in my social services files, it truly tells the story of a woman who had huge issues with food and couldn't take care of me.

Everything that my mother chose to not due she blamed on her health. My mother missed a lot of milestones in my life, and those were times that she could not every get back. I love my mom but it's one of those love hate relationships, and many people stated it was a very toxic relationship. My mother couldn't handle me being successful; she couldn't handle me accomplishing anything. Perhaps it was because of her own insecurities, I truly do not know but my mother was anything but caring towards me.

Starting Grade Seven at Ron Brent Elementary was scary, again I was new to the school, and you'd think I would have become accustomed to the new school thing but in actual reality I hadn't. For me it became another year that I had to attempt make new friends. After all I moved around so much throughout my school years I never had any really close friends, as I hadn't had the opportunities to make them.

School was a very big issue for me, I was dressed nerdy, I always had to wear a boys haircut because of the fact my mother would cut it too short accidently so she claimed, and then would have to cut it short. I was so skinny and I had to wear these red leotards which people would call me spaghetti legs. The kids in my grade seven class bullied me on a daily basis. This one girl named Blendina absolutely tortured me. She would call me names, she would yell at me, say that I was stupid. Another girl, named Rhonda would punch me. Then there was a girl named Cheryl Baker. Cheryl was considered the "BAD GIRL", she stole from stores, she was the tough kid and always got into physical fights. I remember her and I became friends and we would run down to the corner store and steal smokes. During this time the cigarettes were still where the customer could just grab them themselves. We would then head back to the school and smoke. I will always remember the first time I took a puff of smoke, I had sucked in so hard that the filter fell off and I had gotten tobacco in my mouth, and I started coughing so hard I felt like I was going to vomit.

Unfortunately this feeling did not deter me from smoking, I ended up smoking for 24 years before I would decide to quit. I started smoking I think to fit in with the other kids. But anyways we can go back into that later, but I want to tell you about my bully.

I absolutely hated going to school in fact I was terrified to go. My bully Rhonda would beat me up every chance she got. She also would punch me in the face when the teachers were not looking. I remember one time when we had gym and I was in the change room and well they put my clothes into the toilet and I had to walk home in my gym strip. I hated school. It was really bad, I remember this one time I had a big pink duffle bag which I carried my books home, in grade seven your bag can get quite heavy depending on the text books you end up taking home. I would carry this bag home, and it was heavy. This one time the bell had just rung signaling it was three o'clock and that it was the end of the school day. I left the classroom , and I was followed by Rhonda. She had been telling all the girls that I better watch it after school because she was going to beat me up.

I was feeling nervous about going out the door, I was scared she was going to follow me. So I ran out of the classroom without looking back, just as I got onto the grass, I could hear a bunch of kids, yell Rhonda there's Dianna go get her. I turned around and all of a sudden I had this big group of about thirty kids or more surrounding me and Rhonda came into the middle, and pushed me. I just stood there, she then punched me in the face, and I just screamed and cried and didn't want to be there, I yelled "leave me alone", "I don't want to fight you", leave me alone. One of the kids was watching for the teachers, and all of a sudden a boy yelled the principal is coming. Rhonda threw my pink duffle bag on my head as I was laying on the ground bloody and crying. The principal came over and everyone else took off. I didn't say anything and took off home.

This was an everyday thing, fights like this happened on the way home outside the school grounds, on the school grounds, in the girls change room. It was frustrating. I talked to my sister about it and sometimes she would sneak away from the high school early and race up to my school and protect me when she could, but for the most part I was on my own to deal with being bullied. For me being a victim of bullying really affected my school work, I couldn't learn, I was terrified to deal with anything at school I tried to tell my mom about what was going on but I got blamed for it or she didn't believe me what was being done to me. It was always put on me "I must have done something to make these kids not like me", I must have pissed them off. But really the only thing I had issues with was being different. I had to eat different food than everyone else, and I picked my nose and ate it. And then at times I lived in foster homes.

If only the school would have reprimanded my bully I think things would have been a lot easier. At times I wanted to kill myself instead of going to school and face my bully. I couldn't handle the constant name calling and fear of being beat up.

One of my biggest mistakes on how I dealt with my bully is I didn't tell on my bullies, when my teachers asked me what was wrong, I would say nothing. I never told the teachers that I was being picked on I kept it all inside and thought I could deal with it on my own, and I also felt that if I ignored it that it would go away. I was wrong it continued all the way through elementary school. I would encourage people to tell about their bullies, and if you are a parent and your child comes to you and tells you that they are being bullied, and they won't admit it to the school, tape record your child telling you without their knowledge and then take it to the school. It may must solve your bullying issue.

I know that being bullied wasn't my fault it was just that I was different and that kids are mean. So not only did I have to deal with bullying I also had to deal with not having my dad around anymore because he had moved to Vancouver again. My mom met a man named "Corey", and they met at church I think, in any event my mother decided she would marry him. He had two children of his own. Mom and him got married, and that is what sent me packing. My mom accused me of sticking a nail in my step fathers cake, and that I allegedly tried to kill him. Off to Foster Care I went once again, only this time I would spend two years at BLLC before being transferred to the Maples in Vancouver BC.

CHAPTER 7 "THE MAPLES"

It was shortly after my fourteenth birthday when I entered the Maples Adolescent Treatment Center in Burnaby BC. I remember meeting with a woman they called a social worker named Margot. She was the one who showed me around cottage three, and told me that it was a voluntary admission. At the time I went there I was not aware that it was a psychiatric facility for kids who had mental health issues, I thought it was a facility where you go to work on things with your parents. I was wrong. To describe the place the grounds of the facility are gorgeous. However what happened inside the buildings is not so beautiful as the staff of the facility makes it out to be.

At the time I was a resident at the facility, the majority of their funding came from social services but also from private   families.

When conducting research for my book it was brought to my attention that a lot of the policies and procedures have changed over the years and what used to go on does not occur any longer. Since I was a resident as well there had been a change of directors as well as their mandates have changed, and the facility is more focused on the safety of the residents as well as it has very different parameters as to what it had prior. Unfortunately only the residents presently would be able to tell whether or not this is true or not. I cannot say one way or another however, I must state that the new director of the facility was very pleasant to speak with and very caring and sincere. I also found out this Director, worked at the facility during which time I was also a resident. To any person being in such a facility would be scary, now it's more for severely mentally ill youth.

Although, most youth that get sent to the Maples have troubled backgrounds, and generally speaking have had some sort of difficulties with Mental Health issues. I was no exception to this. As a child I sustained a very large number of "LABELS", based on the behaviors I would exhibit in a variety of the placements I resided. The labels such as Attention Deficit Disorder, Attention Deficit Hyperactivity Disorder, Borderline Personality Disorder, Anti-Social Disorder, Psychopathic, Conduct Disorder, Bipolar Disorder, Munchausen's Syndrome, amongst other diagnosis. I was a fourteen year old with some pretty serious labels. Some of the labels I was given most psychiatrists normally would not make such a diagnosis at the age I was. Many of the diagnosis that I had were just because no one knew what was wrong with me.

It became apparent that my relationship with my mom was not good, in fact many psychiatrists stated that they should limit my contact with my mother all together. While residing at the Maples, I was placed in Cottage Three. Under the direction of Barb Stickle (my key worker who was a registered psychiatric nurse) and Margot Stephens and Dr. Sanoto.

The treatment plan for me at the Maples was to help me deal with being previously sexually abused and attend a girls group, as well as deal with relationships all together.

I could not stand the Maples. During my stay there I became really good friends with another girl named Tracy A. She was a short aboriginal girl with dark black hair with it died blonde on top. Her and I got along most days, in fact we ran away a lot as well, and at times she encouraged me to do things that I shouldn't do. One of the things that I did was Overdose on Tylenol, with her. We both didn't like living at the Maples, and it was through her I learned about cutting. I would cut my arms with anything I could find, such as glass, twigs, anything sharp. I truly didn't want to die; I was doing it for attention.

When Tracy and I would run away together we usually hung out under the parking garage of the Sheraton Hotel because at the time there was an old restaurant that had went out of business and they had all the old booth's out there and we would hang out there and sleep on the booths.

I hated the Maples because of the way I was treated. For starters, I was provided medications which there were never any written consents to administer these medications to me. I also noticed a pattern with the psychiatrists that worked at the Maples, they would authorize the nurses to give medications to the individuals who resided there without actually seeing the patient first hand. For example Dr. Sonoto who was my psychiatrist while there (at least according to one of the reports in my file) Would allow my nurse Barb Stickle to administer heavy drugs to me, when it wasn't necessary. The staff at the facility over use the ability of medications, so that they don't have to deal with the individuals behavior. They would consider an individual being agitated just because they didn't want to do a particular activity or because they wanted to leave the center. Heaven forbid you have feelings or emotions and let them out appropriately.

I remember being placed in the Seclusion room on a daily basis for hours at a time with no clothes on, and they would come in and hold me down *Unnecessarily, and shove a needle in my ass full of some medication.* Shortly after this, I remember running around the room in circles staring at the floor, drooling so bad because of the medication, until I got so dizzy I would pass out asleep on the floor. I would then wake up so groggy that I couldn't remember where I was, and when I would realize that I was in the seclusion room I would knock on the door because I had to go to the bathroom and no one would allow me out. I would find a corner of the room to pee in. This was a regular thing that happened to me.

The staff would drug me so that they did not have to deal with me and this was a regular thing. They drugged everyone just because they could. I hated this place with a passion. Another time I had run away I was accused of taking a rock and scratching the staff members car with it. I was criminally charged regarding this but really I didn't do it. Whenever the staff would physically restrain me I would fight back, especially if it was a man trying to strip search me, I was scared, so I would kick at them and hit them and threaten them because I wanted them to leave me alone. I felt so violated with the fact of them looking at me with no clothes on. I understand they felt that I was going to hurt myself only because I had a "LABEL" but truly I had never done anything truly dangerous. It was all superficial. Meaning that if I really wanted to hurt myself badly I could have. If someone is determined to kill themselves they will. No one can stop that person no matter how hard they try to. I found Maples a very messed up place to reside in. Although things have probably changed since I was there I still have ill feelings towards the place.

Looking back at the Maples I feel that I was treated very inhumanely and that they treated all the kids like that. I know numerous times they would handcuff me as well, and at times they would take me to the "PHASE Two" locked down unit. It was really bad. When doing research for my book I was told that policies have since changed, and I don't truly believe it. I know that the facility is under new management, and the woman that ran the organization when I was there is no longer there.

The main issues I had there was with the administration of psychiatric medications that aren't even manufactured for people under the age of 18, also with the endless strip searches. And then of course when you fight back you constantly get charged with Assault and transferred back and forth between the youth jail and the Maples.

I eventually left the Maples and was placed with my father on a short term basis. During the time I lived with my father, I came to realize just how violent he was and how bad he was an alcoholic. He was living with his new girlfriend, and they would get drunk and fight. Sometimes I was so scared that I would hide under my blanket and pretend I was sleeping.

I remember his girlfriend Patsy coming in drunk, she would be yelling at me telling me to do this or that, and I just pretended to be sound asleep. Patsy was scary when she was drunk. What she saw in my father I have no idea, but I can say that my father and her deserved each other. Patsy was nice at times but she sure liked her booze. I remember this one particular night my dad and her went out drinking, they came home and were arguing about the fact that I had my friend Rochelle over still. Rochelle was a runaway from the Maples whom I still kept in contact with. Patsy had told me that Rochelle couldn't stay with us anymore, I ignored her and told Rochelle to ignore her that she was drunk. Patsy took off after yelling at my dad. I went into my dad's room to check to see if he was okay. That is when I saw my dad under the covers and something was moving up and down. I asked him if he was okay. He told me that he was okay and that he had drank some Red Wine, and that he was leaving Patsy. I then asked him what was moving up and down he didn't tell   me.

He did say however he was horny. He told me that I could give him a hand job but that wouldn't be right because I was his daughter, but that I could ask my friend too. I got scared and left the room. A few minutes later my father told me that we were going to his friends house in Deep Cove the next day.

The next day arrived and dad took Rochelle and I to the beer store where he picked up a 6 pack of beer. We then drove through these really windy roads to get to his friends place. Dad started drinking the beer and said that I could have one. I was 15 and I was drinking my first beer. Rochelle started drinking as well with me. By the time we reached my dad's friends place, I was drunk shit all of us were including my father who was   driving.

I must have passed out or something because the next thing I know Rochelle woke me up and was freaking out and told me that my dad had raped her. I freaked we went inside the house, at which time my father and a guy were walking around a pool table, and the guy had punched my father in the nose. My dad was bleeding and he was telling me that we were going to leave. I was terrified.

I ended up leaving with some other guy who was sober with Rochelle, we went and hopped into this guy's truck, and as we were driving away my dad was standing in front of the truck. I was so scared that he was going to hit him with the vehicle, I was also scared that my father was going to hop in our van and drive so drunk. Rochelle and I were taken to a payphone which I used to call social services. I then ended up going into a short term foster home called Short Stop until I could be moved to Prince George. It was at this time that I had tried to call the Jenkins and confront them about what happened to me as a child.

I then moved back to Prince George, and my mother was provided an opportunity to raise me, she declined to take me in. I at that point became a permanent ward of the government and I was placed at BLLC on the Hart Highway once again.

CHAPTER 8 "BLLC"

BLLC was initially considered a "LEARNING FOR LIVING CENTER". It was considered a privately run group home by private people.

I am sure at first the owners Marcel & Sandra had very good intentions, with their facility however they eventually were shut down due to the allegations of abuse that surfaced with respect to their policies and treatment of the children that resided in their facility.

Many of the issues regarding

Marcel & Sandra, were of French decent. Marcel had dark black hair that was poker straight and he allowed his bangs to go into his eyes. He also wore glasses, and was always dressed in a business suit.

Sandra was very sharply dressed as well. She also wore glasses from what I can recall. They had a son named Kevin who also worked at the group home.

BLLC had many policies that created havoc for the residents. For starters they had AWOL policy, this was a policy where if you decided to run away (which I did quite regularly) when you returned to the center (even if you were on the centers property, you had to do what was called a BIG block run. This run to give you an idea was huge. You would turn right onto Foothills Blvd off of Vellencher Drive, then you would follow Foothills Blvd until you get to Chief Lake Road at which time there is a light you would make a right hand turn then you would run down Chief Lake until you see South Kelly Road running parallel to Chief Lake at which time you would Follow South Kelly Road all the way up until you come back to Vellencher Road. You would also have to do two of them during the seven days which you would be forced to stay in your room. During AWOL policy you were not allowed to talk to anyone else in the house.

You ate your meals at different times, you were only allowed to do chores. For the most part you were a prisoner in your room. The other part of AWOL policy was that the staff would bag up all of your belongings including your clothes and place them in lock up in the basement. You were not allowed any of them. Also during the day you were not allowed to lay on your bed because if you did they would take your mattress away from you. I guess they didn't want you to sleep all the time.

So for seven days you would have to stay in your room, at times they would give you lines to write as well, hundreds of them. I usually did them just to have something to-do. If you got caught talking to someone else while you were on a policy you would get them put on the same policy as you. It was rather stupid but it was the fact of life in this house.

They had the other policies as well such as *
Restraint Policy – this was similar to that of AWOL
policy except you had to spend 5 days in your room,
and do a small block run and one big block run. You
were put on this policy if you were physically
restrained by staff at any time. I was placed on this
policy consistently. You would also lose everything
as well. They also had a Threat policy which was 2
days in your room a small block run, and no desert.
You were put on this if you threatened someone.
They also had FIRE policy, this is when you get
caught with matches or a lighter and you also had to
write a report explaining why fire was dangerous to
play with.

Then there was Escort policy, this was when the
staff would walk with you to the time out area which
was conveniently placed under the stair case.

Many of the issues that surrounded the closure of
BLLC was that the staff were utilizing physical
restraint as a way of being close to the residents.

For example Kevin B. the son of Marcel & Sandra,
physically restrained me in the back stairwell. He
used this as a way to touch me inappropriately. I
remember it as if it was yesterday.

I was constantly on restraint policy and escort
policy, because when they told me to go to time out
for stupid reasons I wouldn't go. They also had
swearing policy, if you swear you had to do
hundreds and hundreds of lines. This group home

was horrible. I was there twice once when I was 12 and when I was 15. When I was twelve not too much bad stuff happened or if it did I don't recall very much. The abuse stuff happened more when I was fifteen. When I was twelve I was put in Girl Guides of Canada, I loved it. I finally found a place where I was accepted for who I am. If you have kids and want them to feel accepted an organization like Girl Guides or Brownies, or Cubs is a phenomenal place to put your kids. Not only did I feel like I belonged, I was treated with respect and I started to make some friends but I was also taught on how to be a friend too.

At age fifteen at BLLC, I had a huge incident occur that would change my life forever. I had met a guy named Wayne Gauthier, well I started to date him and he decided to hijack a school bus. It was the middle of winter, and I had ran away with him and was staying with him at his sister's house. He was really big into the dungeons and dragons game. So this one night he gave me a gun. He told me he wanted me to hijack the school bus with him as he had this girl he used to date that he knew would be on it. I got scared as I knew that he had a sawed off rifle under the bed. I made an excuse that I had to go back to the group home and grab some clothes.

I took the b.b. gun with me and walked in the freezing cold weather to the group home, thinking what the fuck was I going to do. Wayne had said that he was going to kill me if I didn't do this bus thing. There was no way that I was going to hijack a bus with kids, I felt I had to get out of this and I didn't know what to do. I did the only thing I could think of. I took the gun with me inside the group home.

The staff saw me just as I entered the downstairs door, and I was told that I had to sit in time out for $\frac{1}{2}$ hour and then I would have to go do a big block run. I didn't want to do this. It was at this point the worker Ed saw the gun I had in the waist band of my pants. I remember him fighting with me over this gun, and I knew that it was not a real gun that it was just a pellet gun which resembled a real gun but he didn't know that.

The owner of the group home just happened to be there and came downstairs to help Ed. They managed to get the gun away from me at which time I took off outside and started running down the road. Just as this happened the police pulled up and arrested me. I was then placed in the youth detention center and charged with possession of a firearm, pointing a firearm and breach of probation (as I had an assault charge from previous because I was being restrained and fought back).

I went to court a few days later and I was ordered to attend the Juvenile Services to the Court, for a psychiatric assessment. I explained to the psychiatrist at this particular place that my boyfriend Wayne, was planning on hijacking a school bus, and I told them about the plan he had. I guess they didn't believe me but about two weeks later, Wayne had in actual fact hijacked the school bus and they got pulled over because they hit a snow bank. The bus was hijacked on February 14, 1990. Wayne, who was 18 at the time and his friends one also 18, and the other 14, took thirteen students and the bus driver hostage, leading the police on a short chase.

Here is an article that appeared in the Prince George Citizen on the twentieth anniversary of the shocking crime given to me courtesy of the Prince George Citizen

PHOTO courtesy of the Prince George Citizen Newspaper

The taking of 212   PART 1
Written by: Rodney Venis and Kyle Storey
Citizen Staff

Twenty years later, a look back at the hijacking of the Hixon school bus

Shortly after the bell rang at schools across Prince George on Feb. 13, 1990, more than 4,000 children and teenagers stepped onto buses bound for home, friends and all points in between.

Most would be in the care of Standard Bus, which at the time held the largest transportation contract in School District No. 57 and carried those 4,000 students on 47 buses that, combined, travelled an estimated
9,656 kilometers per day or around 1.85 million kilometers a year.

Among those 47 was Bus No. 212, which left Prince George secondary school that Tuesday afternoon on its usual run to Hixon.

Its driver, Syl Meise, had clocked up a few of Standard's million kilometers driving 212 and his student passengers – who he liked to call his kids – for seven, uneventful years.

The father of two had already been informed the ride was boring a few weeks prior to that day before Valentine's by a student who vowed to pick up a Walkman to at least add a soundtrack to the dullness.

Both would soon have plenty to get excited about.

Indeed, that day was a little different for Meise when he pulled out of PGSS with 18 kids on board; three teens had talked their way onto his bus claiming they had "a package" for one of his usual charges.

But strange passengers riding school buses weren't unusual at the time – Sharon Zarek, the then district transportation co-coordinator would later tell the Citizen that random students would catch a lift on the district's wheels if they didn't feel like driving, a friend's promise fell through, or they were visiting someone.

However, Chris McGill, a regular on Meise's bus, didn't care for the trio. He thought they looked "really raggedy," and they didn't make eye contact. One of them kept pulling his short jacket over his stomach.

McGill later told the Citizen one of the passengers had supposedly gone out with one of teens (her mother would insist she no longer "hangs around with that boy.")

The teen remarked to Meise that "Oh, she's my old lady" as she got off and added the trio would be leaving a couple stops later.

The 17-year-old McGill got off next, sliding off the pages of Prince George history, leaving Meise, 13 passengers and the three teens on the bus.

That's when Meise remembers, two decades later: an inconspicuous stop past 15 Mile road, "just as we were coming out of the dip at Cale Creek," a few kilometers south of what is now Art Knapp's.

That's when one of the teens – it's unclear if it was an 18-year-old named Wayne George Gauthier or Brad, also 18 – told Meise he had a "sawed-off .303 British" rifle pointed at the back of his head.

(Brad asked his last name not be used due to the attention the incident has brought his family.)

"At first you kind of snicker, you know," said Meise.

"But then I looked back and saw the hammer was cocked.

"At that point, you kind of go numb and think, 'I'm dead.'"

It was 4:30 p.m. that afternoon. Meise, 13 young lives, and Bus No. 212 were now in the hands of a gun-wielding teenager.

School District No. 57 superintendent Jim Imrich would learn, like most of Prince George, what was going on on Meise's bus secondhand.

Like a curious citizen, the district listened to the police scanner and, as Imrich walked by the office switchboard, he was told there was "an incident" involving a school bus.

Moments before Imrich heard the news, Meise had started talking to his rifle-toting captor.

"He kept telling me to shut up, but I kept talking anyways."

He discovered the teens wanted to steal a car and drive it to South America.

Meise managed to convince them nobody owned a vehicle in as small a community as Hixon.

He'd help them steal a ride – in Prince George. The trio agreed and with that Meise turned his bus – and perhaps a tragedy – around.

His fellow drivers couldn't figure out why Bus No. 212 was heading back to Prince George at that time of the day.

Meise's radio crackled to life with calls from them and his dispatcher.

The teens wouldn't let him answer but the driver's silence told everyone something was wrong.

The trio wanted to know if Meise had a car – and he wonders to this day if he should have told the truth.

"I said no, my wife had it at work, which she didn't, but I didn't want them in my yard either," said Meise.

"Maybe we could have ended it sooner but I had two little kids and Linda at

home ..."

He was told to call in and report his bus was under the control of three teens with firearms.

"The dispatcher (Dave Nelson) said, "You're kidding," said Meise.

"At that point (the teen) grabbed the microphone out of my hand and said they were bringing the bus to Sunland Motor Cars and 'If I see any police or cars in the way I'm going to start shooting.'"

Meise realized it was the first time his teen captors, who were fairly calm, had brought up violence.

Standard called the RCMP, which brought the news to the horrified ears of Superintendent Imrich.

"Basically, we could listen in on the RCMP," said Imrich, now retired.
"So we just sat there and listened. We couldn't do anything unusual; there was not much we could do."

But someone else was now within earshot – RCMP Insp. Merv Harrower.

Strangely enough, the taking of a Hixon school bus by gunpoint wasn't too much of a shock to RCMP Insp. Merv Harrower.

At the time, the Prince George RCMP detachment was the third largest in Canada and Insp. Harrower touted the resume one would expect from the operations officer of an 108-member force.

He'd been in charge of the plainclothes unit in Peace River and served as the staff sergeant in charge of major investigations in Calgary.

He'd been in "quite a few of these ERT situations, negotiations and hostage situations."

Indeed, when he assumed inspector duties in Prince George in Dec. 1987, his members faced, over the holiday season alone, 13 incidents involving "barricaded persons", guns, or suicides .

"Prince George had lots of violent crime incidents during the time I worked there," said Harrower, who now works as a consultant after a 30-year career with the force and a stint with the provincial government.

Harrower's approach to hostage-taking situations was straightforward:
stop everything, get it isolated, get things under control and start talking.

"The first thing is to get communication with them, find out what they want or what's going on, then talk to them, start to calm them down, because if you calm them down, the adrenaline kind of slows down and the risk starts to go down," said Harrower.

"The whole idea is to slow the whole thing down ... start a dialogue.

Even if you're shouting back and forth, it doesn't matter."

Luckily, 20 years ago, Meise was thinking the same thing and kept the hostage-takers talking as his bus made its way to Sunland.

Meanwhile, Insp. Harrower directed his officers to block traffic on the route to the car dealership, which was on the corner of 20th Avenue and Vine.

It was a bitter minus-20 as the RCMP evacuated the car dealership, set up a perimeter around the bus and made a nearby service station their command post. The time was about 5 p.m. and Insp. Harrower's detachment had succeeded in containing the situation.

Unfortunately, his Emergency Response Team was en route from Fort St.
James, where they had been conducting a training exercise.

The situation was not ideal for the 13 teens on the bus or Meise.

"To be frank, the average policeman is not in a position to take a shot in a high-risk situation, so you try your very best to avoid that at all cost," said Harrower.

"If (the teens) had shot somebody, we then would have had to rush the bus with the people we had. That's risky, risky stuff."

With that in mind, he turned to the head of his detective squad and main hostage negotiator, Staff Sergeant Elles Peleskey.

PART 2

Standoff at Sunland

On Feb. 13, 1990, RCMP hostage negotiator Elles Peleskey sought to defuse

the hijacking of the Hixon school bus and the taking of 14 people

Rodney Venis and Kyle Storey

Citizen staff

Hunkerered down at a service station near the then Sunland Motor Cars during the late afternoon of Feb. 13, 1990, hostage negotiator and RCMP Staff Sergeant Elles Peleskey prepared to contact three teen gunmen in control of the Hixon school bus.

On board the bus, parked outside Sunland on the corner of 20th Avenue and Vine, were 14 hostages – 13 Prince George secondary school students and bus driver Syl Meise. Their captors were three teenagers – Wayne Gauthier, 18, Brad, 18, and an unidentified 14 year old – wielding two sawed-off rifles.

(Brad asked his last name not be used due to the attention the incident has brought his family.)

The dealership had been cleared while police officers took positions surrounding the bus in minus-20 conditions. The high-powered weapons and elite officers of Prince George's Emergency Response Team – better known as SWAT – were not immediately available as they rushed back to the city from a training exercise in Fort St. James. But that team was a last resort and, if they were needed, it meant Peleskey had failed and the outcome for the hostages at Sunland would be bloody.

An ambulance was standing by if, indeed, that happened.

Shortly before 5 p.m., Peleskey keyed the radio. Twenty years later, he can't recall this particular part of the situation but, according to a source close to the incident, several hostages were close to death.

"The ostensible leader of this outfit ⋯ insisted on being called, I forget what it was, Black Eagle or some damn fool thing," said the source. "All the kids on the bus laughed and damn near got shot for that."

Luckily, the hijackers exercised restraint. They made their demands to Peleskey: a police radio, handcuffs and a fast car – to get them to South America.

It didn't make any sense to the veteran officer – but he hadn't counted on the ingenuity of the driver Meise.

Half an hour previously, one of the hijackers had put a gun to Meise's head and demanded they find a car in Hixon. Meise convinced the gunman no one owned a vehicle in such a small community – and offered to drive him and his confederates to Prince George. The sight of Meise's vehicle, Bus No. 212, returning to the city, contrary to its usual routine, had been enough to alert his fellow drivers something was wrong.

But it left Peleskey slightly baffled: if the hijackers wanted a car to drive to South America, why had they ordered the bus north to Prince George?

"I got the impression that their plans really didn't make sense and these guys didn't really seem to know what they were doing," said Peleskey.

Regardless, the hijackers narrowed down their demands: a white Pontiac Trans Am parked in the Sunland lot.

Unfortunately, the owner, Mike Handsor of Quesnel, hadn't left the keys at the dealership (Handsor would later quip: "I wanted to trade it in, not give it away") and the police weren't in the mood to have the group barreling through Prince George in a high-performance car.

The police started to position sharpshooters and told the gunmen they couldn't give them the Trans Am.

Thirty-eight minutes into the standoff, the call went out for more police officers, to be placed in reserve if the standoff dragged on in the frigid cold.

The police dug in for a siege.

For a while, Stacy Leboe (nee Colebank) says she got nervous if somebody raised something – especially something long – quickly or sharply near her.

It reminded her of guns – and the hostage taking.

She'd been riding Bus No. 212 since Grade 8 – and was now trapped outside of Sunland.

Her primary recollection is a student with glasses, Flint Keil, who helped the driver calm the hijackers down. "I don't remember what words he used," she said.

Regardless, her part in the ordeal was about to end.

At 5:48 p.m. the teens agreed to release Leboe and another female student, Bonny Borutski, so they could go to the bathroom.

That's when Leboe's mother, Barb Colebank, thinks she saw a TV news report about the Hixon school bus and saw her daughter being let off.
"I'm sure it was something to do with the bathroom," said Colebank.

Leboe and Borutski were supposed to return with handcuffs and a radio.
The RCMP didn't let them go back to the bus.

The bus driver, Meise, meanwhile, was trying to conduct his own negotiations with the gunmen, offering to trade himself for all the hostages.

"[I was] told [by the hostage takers] they couldn't take me because I had young children and I was needed at home."

A few minutes after Leboe and Borutski were released, the bus started to edge towards a 1988 Subaru. A student told the Citizen that the hijackers got their teen hostages to pick out an alternate getway car.
At 5:55 came a new request — the hijackers wanted to go to Dawson Creek. Five minutes later, a Grade 12 hostage, reportedly a friend of the hijackers, was chosen to go with them.

The offer got the senior officer at the incident, RCMP Insp. Merv Harrower, thinking.

Letting the hijackers loose went against the conventional doctrine of keeping such situations contained.

But what if he let the hijackers have their car — and left it running near the bus, draining the gas tank.

Harrower arranged spike belts and pursuit cars in preparation for a high-speed chase. He also began cutting Prince George off. He summoned officers from Mackenzie and Quesnel, armed with spike belts, as a last line of defence and installed his members on every exit to the city.

He had so many officers deployed throughout the community that, at 6:02 p.m., the detachment ran out of shotguns.

Harrower then arranged to have a spotter plane follow the hijackers when they did receive their vehicle.

Officers dispatched to the homes of Wayne George Gauthier and Brad had discovered the teens had been planning the hijacking and had sawed-off the barrels of two rifles – a .303- and .22-calibre weapon – in their parent's basement.

"Their parents were pretty shocked, the whole town was in shock," said Harrower.

A half-an-hour later, the bus started to move – just as Prince George's Emergency Response Team reached the city at 6:35 p.m.

One of the hostage takers emerged from the bus, moved a car, and returned to the bus.

Finally, the police released the Subaru – which had been running as Harrower ordered – in exchange for all but one of the hostages. The driver Meise was told to take it to the bus.

"He said you go get that car and you better come back or I'll start shooting," said Meise.

Using the bus driver as a shield, the gunmen and the hostage got into the car and drove slowly away at 6:40 p.m.

Around a minute later, the Prince George ERT stormed the school bus.

'I'll see you in hell'

The taking of school bus No. 212 ends after a chase on the Hart Highway

Rodney Venis and Kyle Storey

Citizen staff

A wrong turn down a dead-end road in a getaway car running out of gas.

That's how the hijacking of school bus No. 212 ended at 7:05 p.m. on Feb. 13, 1990.

Four hours earlier, three teens had gotten onto the bus at Prince George secondary school with two sawed-off rifles wrapped in a wall hanging. At 4:30 p.m. the reported ringleader, Wayne George Gauthier, put gun to the head of driver Syl Meise and announced he was taking control of the bus.

An around hour-and-a-half standoff with police had ended around 6:40 p.m. with the three teens and a hostage driving away with a maroon 1988 Subaru. The price of the car was 11 student hostages and Meise.

But Gauthier would decide to turn down what was then Wright Creek Road after leading police up the Hart Highway. He realized too late it was a dead end, spun the car around — and saw his windshield view filled by two oncoming police cars. Soon, they were surrounded.

"You've got 30, 40 different shotguns in a half circle around the car,"
said a hostage taker named Brad who asked, these 20 years later, his last name not be used.

"I looked at Wayne as he was getting out of the car and said, 'I'll see you in hell.'"

On the other hand, Const. Gary Godwin felt like hell.

That Feb. 13 marked the final day of a three-day outdoor survival training exercise for Prince George's RCMP Emergency Response Team.
Designed to test whether Godwin and the seven other members of the ERT could track a suspect in the roughest of wilderness, the constable had spent most of the past 48-plus hours either on snowshoes or sleeping in a snow cave near Fort St. James.

"Waking up in the morning was a bit chilly," admitted Godwin.

That afternoon was likewise spent on snowshoes as the ERT did compass work in the heavy snow and bitter February cold.

At around 4:30 p.m., "well into the exercise," said Godwin, the call came in over the ERT's radio.

A school bus had been hijacked and 14 hostages were under the control of three armed teenagers. Prince George's ERT would be needed.

The fatigued officers snowshoed back to their vehicles. Godwin and another officer broke out the gear from the team's van, dispensing MP5 submachine guns and special-issue nine-millimetre Sig Sauer semi-automatic pistols. Most of the team hopped into more manuverable Chevy Suburbans, racing the hour-and-a-half to Prince George over winter roads.

Godwin, the team's sniper, and the other officer lumbered back to the city in the van. It meant the police officers surrounding bus No. 212, parked outside the then Sunland Motors on 20th Avenue, were facing a band of teen gunmen with only .38 pistols and shotguns.

At 6:40 p.m., in exchange for all but one of the hostages, the three teen gunmen extracted from police a 1988 maroon Subaru and left Sunland, heading north.

At 6:41 p.m., with the hijackers fleeing, Prince George's ERT

arrived — and stormed the school bus. "That's when I lost it," said Meise. "They were loud and abusive, worried that there might still be hijackers on the bus. I wasn't very nice at that point."

RCMP Insp. Merv Harrower, who was in charge of the Prince George detachment at the time, is still a little chagrined — but not quite apologetic — about that part of the incident.

"I can understand some of the kids thought, 'Oh, we're safe' and then, all of sudden, these guys with black toques and everything come roaring in," said Harrower. "Of course, the (ERT's) adrenaline is going at 100 miles an hour, they just come roaring back, they get here too late and everybody's left. I ended up apologizing all over the place for that. What happened, we weren't sure there wasn't anybody else left on the bus, right?

"How do you know? When you saw the hostages in Columbine, everyone came out with their hands on their head, even the students, right? Because you really don't know if you've got somebody hiding amongst the students."

Then-school board superintendent Jim Imrich had both praise for the RCMP, Staff Sergeant Elles Pelleskey, the hostage negotiator — and Meise. He couldn't remember if he talked to the bus driver that night or the next day.

"I just said thank you so much for being so calm and cool."

Accolades could wait — at the time, Insp. Harrower was more concerned with the Subaru racing over the John Hart Bridge.

He'd left the Subaru running near the bus, draining its gas tank, throughout the standoff. He surrounded the city with police officers and had RCMP from Quesnel and Mackenzie on the highway as a second line of defence. A spotter plane was tracking the hijackers.

He had a spike belt ready to put an end to a chase. But events would throw a monkey wrench into his plans.

"Why they turned north I don't know," said Harrower. "You know how these things develop, they develop so quickly and we didn't get the spike belt pulled across the road in time, that's why they got across the bridge. But we had an aircraft up and they were being monitored."

That's when the hijackers realized the Subaru didn't have much fuel.
But Harrower had one more card to play.

"We also had the service stations shut down on that road north," he said.

The Subaru pulled into the Birchill Drive Turbo gas station. Harrower's scheme wasn't needed — the hijackers couldn't work the lever-operated cap on the Subaru's tank.

"They got down twice and fiddled around under the steering wheel but they simply could not get the tank open," Tammy Munn, a station attendant, told the Citizen. "Then the cops came tearing up behind us and yelled at me to get out of the way, so I did."

The car proceeded up the Hart Highway, turned on the Wright Creek Road but then the hijackers realized it was a dead end.

"The plane was watching them, saw them turn off on a road, went down the road, turned around and they were coming back towards the highway when we decided, I decided, that the thing was getting too risky, I couldn't afford to have a high-speed chase," said Harrower. "I didn't want anyone else hurt, so we took them down, we blocked the road with a car.

"I can remember it was just horribly, horribly icy, and they were on a bit of an incline hill, we went tearing down the hill to grab them, arrest them as quick as we could, and we just slid on the ice all the way up to the car. I was glad no one was hurt, actually."

At 7:09 p.m., the call came in to the Prince George detachment: "Suspects in custody, no injuries."

Arrested were Wayne George Gauthier, 18, Brad, 18, and a 14-year-old teen whose identity still has not been disclosed. They were carrying the .303 rifle and a .22 rifle, both sawed off.

Brad was sentenced to three years for his role in the taking of bus No.

212. Court heard Gauthier recruited him the night before the incident and that, if he refused to participate, his family would be harmed.

Gauthier was sentenced to four years in part because, according to Crown prosecutor John Sutton, "I hesitate to say Gauthier is the brains behind the plan."

The scheme, found in a blue duotang, was: steal a sports car, go to Vanderhoof, then to Queen Charlotte City, committing robberies along the way. After finding "mates" along the way to "bear their children,"
Gauthier hoped to secure two speedboats, race to the Panama Canal and raise an army.

His army would attack small villages and take slaves, eventually building a fortress and a surrounding village.

Court heard Gauthier concocted the plan while smoking marijuana and injesting PCP, otherwise known as angel dust.

PART 4

Hijacker recalls 'that day'

Rodney Venis and Kyle Storey

Citizen staff

Holding his two-year-old son in his arms, a one-time teen gunman is ready to speak.

It was Feb. 13, 1990 when Brad, Wayne George Gauthier, and a still unnamed 14-year-old took control of a school bus and 14 hostages by gunpoint. (Brad asked his last name not be used due to the attention the incident has brought his family.)

He says he's been out of the judicial system since 1998 and drug-free for 13 years. But he knows that doesn't change a hijacking that shocked Prince George and culminated in a three-hour standoff and police chase that led eventually to Brad's arrest.

The father of four wonders how to express how much he regrets what he did 20 years ago.

"God, if there was a way to change this, what I had done, I would do it in a heartbeat, and there's no way on God's green earth, if time could be changed back, that I would have done something like this, because I know how much it's hurting me to have this come back on me," said Brad.
"I can't imagine how it feels for the people that were on that bus, I can't feel enough emotion."

Brad says he met Gauthier, the reported ringleader of the bus hijacking plot, a few weeks before the incident. Gauthier's brother introduced him to the hostage-taker and Gauthier in turn introduced him to the horse tranquilizer ketamine — or, as it's known on the street, Special K.

Brad, 18 at the time, ran away from home and started living in the same house as Gauthier. Soon after, Gauthier told Brad "he wanted to do something that no one else had ever done before in Prince George."

"(He told Brad and the unidentified teen) if you come with me we can go get women across the ocean and all this crap and of course you're high on drugs, so it was, oh, right on, good idea."

The plan, a court would later hear, was to steal a car, rob their way to the Queen Charlotte Islands, buy speed boats, head to the Panama Canal, raise an army on the Amazon River, capture slaves, build a fortress and establish a village.

— from page 1

Originally, said Brad, Gauthier planned to commit the crime with his girlfriend. Instead, he persuaded Brad by threatening to "kill every last one of my family members."

"I told him that I'm not really into threats but if you're willing to kill the rest of my family I guess I gotta do what you say," said Brad.

He watched Gauthier saw the barrel off a .303 rifle with a bare hacksaw blade and then he did the same with a .22 rifle.

He wrapped both in a wall hanging, with one end tied with rope and the other with a belt.

Then, on that Tuesday 20 years ago, he, Brad, and the unnamed teen waited at a bus stop in the Hart to head downtown.

"He tells the driver when he gets on the city bus that (the package) is a camera stand," said Brad.

At the time, Brad says he was under the influence of four drugs — ketamine, pot, cocaine and "six or seven" hits of acid. That was his state of mind when the trio got onto bus No. 212 at Prince George secondary school shortly after 3 p.m.

The bus driver Syl Meise, asked Gauthier about his bundle and was given the same answer – it was a camera stand or tripod.

Two students got off the bus, which was en route to Hixon. Then, near Cale Creek, close to what's now Art Knapp, Gauthier rested the .303 on Meise's shoulder.

"The driver kept going like that," he said with a shoulder-brushing gesture. "He thought it was one of the students playing around – finally the driver looked behind him to say stop that, and there's a
303 sticking in his face."

Brad said the 14-year-old held the other gun, the .22, first, but got tired of brandishing, handed it to Brad and pulled out a large knife, "like a machete."

Gauthier, meanwhile, convinced by Meise there were no cars to steal in Hixon, ordered the bus turned around. Other drivers, alarmed by school bus No. 212 deviating from its usual route, alerted police.

Gauthier demanded the bus go to what was then Sunland Motor Cars, on 20th Avenue (now Gustafson's Kia). Police surrounded the bus, triggering an hour-and-a-half long standoff.

"(The police) told us at any given time they could have plucked us like chickens in a coop," said Brad. "I said, really, why let it go on for so many hours? I was told the only reason they didn't do it was they didn't know which kid it was doing the hijacking. I can see the cops'
point."

Gauthier wanted a fast car, handcuffs and a police radio. Halfway through the siege, he let two students go.

Brad, meanwhile, said he sat by a female and male student with the .22 unloaded.

"I sat halfway on the bus, pulled the clip out, put it on the seat and made sure there were no bullets in the gun," said Brad. "I put the gun on my lap and sat there talking to a girl and guy. Of course, they're scared – I had hair down to here, dressed raggedy, looked like someone who would do something like that. Of course they're worried, there's a guy up there who doesn't look like he's all there and he's got a high-powered rifle."

Brad let them in on a secret.

"I told them if he pulls that trigger that gun will blow up in his face," he said. "When you saw off a gun, you're supposed to taper the end – and if you don't taper the end, when you're cutting the metal, the metal folds in. Basically the bullet blows up in the chamber."

Gauthier secured his car – a maroon 1988 Subaru – in exchange for the release of 10 student hostages and the driver Meise.

They set off north, with the unnamed teen and Brad in the back with a
.22 and one hostage.

The RCMP left the car running, draining most of its gas, and blocked off the city. A plane was following the trio and the hostage. Then Gauthier, hurtling up the Hart, took a turn on Wright Creek Road — a dead end.

The police surrounded and arrested them all when Gauthier tried to turn around.

Brad would plead guilty to a suite of charges and sentenced to three years in jail.

He would encounter Gauthier in jail and claimed the two would fight often before they were separated.

He would spend the next decade in and out of jail. But, eventually, he would start a family and settle down.

He had hoped to start a reconciliation with his family, who he became estranged from after the incident.

"Now, for the rest of my life I'm going to pay for it, no matter if I try to raise a family or not."

Teach me to date some crazy guy who decides that he is wanting to get even with his ex-girlfriend because she dumped him a few weeks prior. It's always amazing how people get so out of sorts over a breakup.

Wayne was very big into the game Dungeons and Dragons, no offence to that game but everyone that I have ever met who plays it are pretty demented. It most certainly has brought people out of the woodwork that are less than desirable. The other thing that blew me away as well as in the article it stated that Wayne was into drugs, I can honestly say when I knew him, he didn't do drugs, at least he didn't come across as a person that did drugs. He just seemed like a guy who wanted to have friends but was a loner. I was the girlfriend that they referred to in the article.

What I saw ofWayne was that he was an exceptional artist, he created blue prints of a house that he wished to build one day. This was the compound that was references in the article. Years later I met him in 2006 again. He was living in an apartment near my house that I was renting close to paddlewheel park. I had just moved into my house when I looked up and saw a guy with long blonde hair and very skinny with tons of tattoos on his arms wearing a tanktop. I asked him who he was and he told me who he was he said he was Wayne Gauthier, I started shaking thinking oh my fucking god he's here years later to kill me. He quickly left just as fast as he appeared. Why he came over that day and how he knew exactly which house I lived in is beyond me. I found out he walked down my street listening to his walkman on a regular basis it was part of his ritual. Nothing happened after that day, and I disassociated with him as well. He was not a part of my life, although we were so close to getting married I am glad we didn't.

What he did to the kids on the school bus was scary considering he could have actually killed me if I hadn't took the gun to the group home and gotten myself arrested. I told the police two weeks before the hijacking that he was going to do it but they didn't believe me.

Chapter 9 "Youth Detention"

When I was transferred to the holding cells by the police I was scared. You are probably thinking to yourself I deserved it after all I did take a gun to the group home. You're probably right, however, it was a pellet gun not a real gun, and also, what would have you done in my shoes? No one believed me about Wayne hijacking the school bus, I told the police three weeks before he did it that he was going to do it but no one believed me.

I was placed in the back of the police car, and transported to the RCMP holding cells. At which time I was handcuffed behind my back. Of course I was tiny frail and looked a lot younger than my age and the handcuffs were on tight but I was able to slip out of them. I didn't however, as I was told if I did that they could charge me with escaping lawful custody.

Unsure as to what I was being charged with exactly, I was sitting in the back of the car. We pulled up into the underground parking where a garage door opened up and then the police officer drove in with the garage door thing coming down behind. The officer got out of the car and placed his gun inside a lock box that was up on the wall and then came and opened the backdoor of the car allowing me out. I then had to follow him into a small elevator where he pushed a button. The elevator doors closed, and then reopened and all I could see is metal bars which created the cells. The cop walked me to the booking area, took a picture of me, and then fingerprinted me and then a woman took over and searched me, then took me into one of the empty cells, and asked me to walk in it. I walked into the cell and the door slid closed behind me making a very loud clanging sound behind. Once in the cell I looked around at my new surroundings, I noticed some scratched writing on the cement wall just beside a set of bunk beds. The beds were made of dark black cold metal and had a very thin rubber mattress shoved on them. There was a silver toilet with very little water and a tiny little metal basin sink. Both were ice cold. The room was entirely constructed out of cement that was painted a baby blue color. The door was made of bars with a little rectangle where it turned out they shove food through to feed you. When the door closes you can hear a very loud clanging and everything echoes. It is a very terrifying feeling being all alone in an isolated cell away from humanity.

Here I was in the cells, terrified, scared, I was 15 in age but not in maturity. I was a very impressionable kid, not too sure what to make of this jail cell experience. I sat in this cell for what seemed hours, all I had was this little metal bed with a 1 inch mattress to sit on , with a horse blanket, I call it a horse blanket because it was extremely rough and so small that it didn't even keep you warm. Several hours later, the woman came back and told me I was being transferred to see a Justice of the Peace. I was marched to this window at which time a woman looked at me looked at some papers on her desk then said that she was remanding me in custody (jail) for court the next morning. This process took all of two minutes, before I was marched back to the cell that I had just came from.

It appeared that I was spending the night, so I laid down on the hard mattress thingy and somewhat fell asleep freezing. The next morning the sheriffs came and picked me up, handcuffed me and placed me into a sheriffs van to transport me to the court house.

If you have never been in a sheriffs van let's just say you don't want to be especially if you are claustophobic . The sheriffs van is made up of little compartments which they place each person they are transporting in. The compartments are fully enclosed with plexi-glass so you can't send things back and forth between inmates. There is however a little crack from the floor up to where the glass starts, and this is how inmates who smoke transfer smokes back and forth without the sheriff seeing.

I arrived at the court house and was placed in a holding cell with a couple of girls who were also kids my age. One girl was in there because she got caught shoplifting, and the other girl was arrested for assault. So we sat there for hours waiting for the sheriff to come get whoever was up next. You could end up waiting for the majority of the day to have your five minutes in court. Its rather frustrating as well because you have no idea how much time has passed as there is no clocks, and sometimes you end up being isolated with no one else in your cell because they have taken your cellmates with them to go to court and don't bring them back.

Waiting for court in the holding cells is frustrating because sometimes you think that the sheriffs forgot about you or that everyone is gone home especially if you are there at the end of the day. It gets so quiet and your terrified that your there by yourself, you think to yourself what if there is a fire? What if no one is here and they forgot about me. It's pretty crazy thinking but they did forget people in the cells before. In fact they even put me in a cell with guys by mistake, the guys thought it was cool, that is of course until I started screaming.

Now it was my turn, you could hear the sheriff walking down the corridor with his keys, walking up to my cell door and puts his key in the door, and yells "Davidson", "Court", I walked out of my cell and followed the sheriff to another door which he turned his key in the door and opened , I walked through the door and found myself sitting in the prisoners box inside the courtroom of Prince George Provincial Court.

The judge was sitting behind a big solid wood desk wearing her judges robe black with a red stripe down each shoulder. I look around the court room and I see the Crown Counsel Prosecutor read the details of my offence to the judge at which time the judge turns to me and asks me if I am pleading guilty or innocent. Not represented by a lawyer, but want to get this shit over and done with , I plead guilty, after all I did take a gun up to the group home, even though it was a pellet gun. I apologize and tell the judge that I am sorry. The judge sentences me to three months in open custody at the Prince George Youth Detention Center, and two years probation with mandatory psychiatric counseling.

I then get whisked away back through the little door and taken back to my holding cell until I am transported to the Prince George Regional Correctional Center which was much later .

The Sheriff attends my cell once again and takes me and handcuffs me and takes me to the sheriff van which is going to be used to transport me to the youth detention center.

After about a twenty minute drive we reach the jail, at which time the sheriff helps me out of the cramped small space of the sheriff van, which I was locked into.

The Sheriff walks me up still handcuffed behind my back up to the doors of the jail. I walk in following like a puppy dog, into a room that has this long counter and I am told to stand in a holding cell thing that has a door that is wide open. So I comply with the directions. The Sheriff dumps his paperwork on the desk and a woman in a blue uniform heavy set walks up grabs the paperwork, and the two chit chat for a bit. The Sheriff then leaves and this woman walks up to me, Okay Davidson, I need you to get undressed and go in here and shower with this kwelda soap, and then get changed into these grey sweat pants and this t-shirt.

I comply and realize this soap stinks to high heaven. When I ask what it's for afterwards the guard doesn't really answer me. When I'm done showering she hands me a blanket, a couple changes of clothes including underwear (all with the PGYCC stamps on them) , and all my clothes and personal effects went into this big yellow envelope and now belonged to them. She then asks me to stand up against the wall so she could search me, Odd considering I just had a stupid shower, so I allowed her to do this, like I really had a choice. When she was finished sticking her hands in places no one wants them to be, she told me to follow her.

We walked down a corridor, and she pushed a button on the wall and said something and asked to be let in then you would hear an air sound and the door would be opened.

I was now standing in a unit, and I was walked to what at first looked to be just a bedroom until I noticed they could actually lock you in the room. Which is exactly what was done to me for the first 24 hours until they got to know me. Looking at my surroundings I saw that there were 5 cell like rooms with a big metal door with a little square window in the middle of it that can lock you in from the outside, then there was a bathroom, a boys television room, a girls television room it was a coed place. Then there was a Guard station with a long almost reception desk looking thing and a room right behind it that had a plexi glass window and metal door called the Time Out room.

What was very strange about this unit was that if they can lock you in your cell why would they need a time out cell? There was also a dining area. The rules here were simple, you do your programs, you do your school work, and you don't get physical with other inmates, if you do you'll find yourself locked into your room, for 24 to 48 hours, with nothing to do. Remember this was jail, not a group home, we didn't even have books on the unit, and it was privilege to have a pencil and paper, like who would I write to anyways. I know my mom never wrote me let alone would allow me to write her. Perhaps my childhood would have been better if my mother would have accepted me.

So they had a CODE system in this jail it's to signify to other guards the level of help needed if a situation were to arise. For example Code 1 is they require an extra staff member but there is no rush because it hasn't escalated yet. Code 2 is a fight between two inmates, Code 3 is when a guard is at risk of getting hurt, or they need backup immediately and a Code 4 is a riot, escape, or suicide. I was always having code 2 called on me I had a code 4 called on me a couple of times because I would threaten suicide.

One thing I learnt quite quickly while spending my time in the Youth Containment Center, was it was safer to start a fight if you heard someone was going to beat you up. This was because then you are in control of the situation. I did this with this one girl Melody P. She was in jail in fact she had always been in jail, I ran into her not only at PGYCC but I had also ran into her previously in the Willingdon Detention Center in Vancouver. So well she just happened to be in this unit that I was just placed in. I had heard she was going to beat me up, for the sake of beating me up. So I walked up to her and pushed her, I made sure that there was more than one guard on the unit in case this bitch got the upper hand. I pushed her and told her I had heard she wanted to fight. She looked at me like oh shit. I told her to go fuck herself and that she was not going to sucker punch me in the television room like I had heard. The fight was on , the guards eventually broke us up and we were both handcuffed and thrown into our adjacent cells. I ended up being locked down for 48 hours and she got 24 hours. They came in a little while later and removed the handcuffs and allowed me out to go to the bathroom. I had to eat in my room and that was about it.

I got into a lot of fights at PGYCC, mainly because I hated it there and this Melody girl consistently picked on me. I remember one time one of the guards Mr. Campbell, who was a much larger man, was watching us in the Gymnasium, this was one of our programs. He did not like people who used vulgar language, I had used the F word for whatever reason and he told me that when I get back to the unit I was going to be locked down for four hours. Of course this started the argument, I told him there was no way I didn't do anything so I swore whatever, and I flipped right out on him and pushed him. He called a code and then I ended up being handcuffed and yanked out of the gym and dragged to the time out room in the unit. I continue to throw a fit, and started booting at the door and screaming that I was going to kill this Melody P. person and that it was a big mistake and I swore a ton. They then decided to move me off the unit and place me in   a   unit   called   SEG.

I had no idea what this was and before I knew it I was being yarded down the corridor by two guards cuffed behind my back (remember I was 14), until will we came to this room that had all plexy glass doors, and I was asked to change into these green coveralls. I said no way was I going to change in front of them (they were male), they took a pair of scissors and cut the clothes off of me and threw me in the coveralls. Then threw me inside this SEG unit.

It was at this time a counselor I knew named Peter Clugston, was working for Forensic Psychiatric Out services or something like that, and he came and visited me, I was locked down in SEG for the last two weeks of my stay.

I ended up in SEG numerous times. My only issues at this facility was that they handcuffed me, and at one time they hogtied me consistently for a period of a week, and left me like that for several hours. They would handcuff me then tie my legs to the cuffs and put a hockey helmet that was three sizes too small. To me I believe this is abuse. I truly was not a danger to myself or anyone else, I was tiny. I was lucky if weighed 80 pounds soaking wet. I also wasn't really suicidal I was just mad. I was mad at the world. Simple as that. During this stage of my life everything was not fair, and being stuck in a situation where two male guards were cutting my clothes off of me I believe that was unacceptable.

I remember one guard Annie Thuveson, she was a long time correctional guard, she too I had seen both while I was in the Prince George Jail as well as the jail in Vancouver (when I was on remand). She beat the shit out of me with my hands handcuffed behind my back.

What is really sad is society needs to treat Juveniles like Juveniles that is of course, if the crime they commit is minor. And I wasn't treated like that. I was treated like a piece of shit that didn't matter. People seriously need to look into that facility, however, I do think things have changed as, as an adult I got a tour and it appeared that none of the units were even used anymore, in fact the unit I was shown was empty. I do know that I met a guard that I really liked, named Whitney Prouse, he was cute, and anytime he worked there, I was as good as gold. A couple times he got to do my ½ hour exercise out in the yard when I was in SEG. I met him at a bar when I was an adult and he was just as cute but he was a pig. Simple as that he had no manners, and again I was drunk at the time so what did the impression I have as an adult really amount too. Distorted I think due to alcohol.

I was released when I was just after my sixteenth birthday but this time to Browndale Care Society in Vancouver BC, after all the gun incident really didn't sit well with the staff and they didn't want me back, I don't blame them. After all I did have a habit of burning out every place I lived.

It was now time for me to live a normal life, and I guess Social Services believed that I could achieve this with Browndale Care Society in Vancouver. According to my records, it appears that my life started to straighten out quite a bit at the time I moved to Browndale.

Chapter 10 "BROWNDALE CARE SOCIETY"

Shortly, after my release from custody, I was moved to West Vancouver, to a house called Ambleside House. It was located on Duchess Avenue in one of the wealthiest neighborhoods of the Lower Mainland, just steps from both the beach and the police station. It was here that I ended up going to regular school West Vancouver Senior Secondary to be exact. However, prior to the school year commencing I had to attend a camping trip that was a month and a half long called Roberts Lake. I guess Roberts Lake was a place the staff at Browndale Care Society went to on a regular basis   every   year.

Roberts Lake was on the Vancouver Island. It was only accessible by boat. So we had to go over in several different boat trips, so that all of us could get over to the camp. What was unique about the camp was that they had these big wooden poles which we would use a piece of wood and nails to pound black dark tarp paper around it so it resembled a shelter like a tent. It was kind of neat from what I recall. The other thing I remember about this camp, is I was a smoker so the lighters the staff would have around their neck on string and we would have to ask them for a light. I also remember that Sandy Coffin, who was my key worker also had my ventolin inhaler on a string which she gave me when I needed it. I loved it there at times. I remember one incident I ran away with another kid, and we went and hiked up to the boat landing two of the staff followed us, but one of the older kids decided to break into a car, and steal alcohol that was in it. He was criminally charged for breaking into the car, however I was treated as a witness according to the reports I found in my Social Services File.

During my time at Ambleside, I found that I learned a lot about camping. I learned how to build an outhouse, I know how to do a lot and it was fun.

After the camping trip we went back to the Mainland and I settled into the house life. For the most part I ran away quite a bit at first mainly because I was trying to avoid issues. I had become friends and had to share my room with Julie T. and she was my friend one night and mean the next. We ran together, I remember one time we ran away and climbed up on the roof of the Shell Gas Station which was directly across the street from Binos Restaurant and the police station we would yell " hey piggy piggy piggy" and make oinking noises." I remember one time Julie ran inside the stations double doors, and dropped a Pink stuffed pig, she was screaming " I smell bacon I smell pork run piggy run because I have a fork" then tossed it into the police station. Things stupid kids do. What we didn't know as we exited that there was a stairway right there and well this big ass cop came out of it and grabbed us and arrested us. No charges were ever laid but let's just say us being annoying little kids was big and this cop didn't take it very lightly as to the harassment we were doing on the police.

This cop supposedly stuck his Billy club up Julies you know what but that was never confirmed. We got in a lot of shit over all of that. We were stupid little teenagers playing games. Simple as that.

Julie and I were good friends while living at Browndale, as an Adult I tried to find her but no luck I think she married but not sure. During my residence at Ambleside House I worked at Lickity Split which was a local ice cream parlor, it was at this time I met a person that just knowing him would change my life forever Michael Berry. I also attended grade 10 at West Vancouver Senior Secondary School. I loved West Van High, during this time I got a job at the West Vancouver Library shelving books. I also became friends with Carly R, and was tutored by a grade twelve guy that I had the hots for named Lorne Hoover. I met Lorne in the hallway when he was closing his locker, I had heard he was really good at math, and I needed a tutor in math because I sucked at it. I asked him if he would be willing to tutor me. He said sure, truly I didn't want help in math I had the hots for him and wanted to date him. It was kind of funny because I don't think he ever clued in. I would go to his house and his mom would bake these awesome cookies and snacks for us while we did my math. I couldn't really concentrate on my math because here I had a guy with short brown hair tall and gorgeous sitting right beside me. It's too bad him and I never got together. He would get together with me as well at the local ice arena where he was a nice person. After Ambleside house, I was moved to Eaton House in

Lynn Valley , part of North Vancouver. It was a house that is designed for semi-independent living.

At Eaton House, is where I met my first boyfriend Michael Hendricks. He lived with his grandparents on Zero Avenue in Langley BC. I am unsure how we actually met. Michael had bleach blonde hair blue eyes, and was gorgeous. We would hang out on the sky train and just ride it all night and kiss. We would cuddle on the sky train . We also went to his grandparents place on a number of occasions. I remember he had a friend named Rob who lived next door to him who I also liked. I remember one night I snuck Michael into the Eaton House and hid him under my bed. I got caught with him in my room of course, and got in trouble. But for the most part I was starting to straighten my life out. Besides my schooling I also, had the opportunity to tutor a grade 4 student at the local library in his subjects. I really enjoyed this responsibility.

During the time I lived at BrownDale, I was also allowed to work as the secretary at the Browndale office, I was able to answer phones and stuff. Also Warren O'Brian who was the director a the time had also got me a job at a clothing factory which his wife worked at. I became the youngest stock taker in Canada. In a nutshell, I was 14 and I was making $18.00 per hour counting rolls of fabric. It was the most easiest job ever. The downfall of the job was that it was in a very bad neighborhood Main & Hastings to be exact which was close to Pigeon Park. (This area has made it on the news for being the highest drug affiliated area in British Columbia.) Regardless of the area, it was work. I liked it.

While living at Eaton House I did run into some difficulties. There were reports that I was being "assaultive", and I was booted out of the house for the night. I would end up calling the afterhours help line because I was not knowing where I should go stay. I eventually would be let back in the house.

One thing that became apparent to me was that the Group Homes were allowed to kick the children out of them. This again I felt was not appropriate. I may have been fourteen but I truly didn't have the skills to live on the street either.

Chapter 11 "The Foster Home from Heaven"

I was now on my way to graduation, not only a high school graduation but also to the graduation out of the government care system. The next two years in care were designed to teach me skills.

To start off I was placed with a very wonderful couple that I honestly believe to this day that if I had been placed with them early on, I would have actually had the opportunity to have a normal child hood. Although I put Jim and Lawanda through hell with my talking in my sleep, as there was an incident where I had threatened to kill them in my sleep, and Lawanda could hear me rustling around, and too her it sounded like I was looking for something this was according to a report she wrote for the Ministry. Then there was some typical teenager stuff, such as experimenting with pot, drinking and smoking and of course staying out late. I have absolutely nothing bad to say about this wonderful couple. I thank god every day that they were put in my life except they should have been put in my life much earlier. I can honestly say I believe it was due to their guidance that I managed to graduate high school. Lawanda was firm with me but she was very respectful.

What I saw in the Tazelaar household, was a normal everyday family. This was something that was never role modeled to me as a child. When Jim and Lawanda would have their adult arguments, there was no fighting between them, they both communicated very efficiently.

I think back to the time I lived with them, and truly I feel bad about how the placement broke down. I know I talk in my sleep, still do to this day, however, truly I would never have done anything to hurt them. They showed me what a real family was like and I hope they know that I truly appreciated all that they had done for me. They are the only family in this book that I did not change the names of mainly because they were such wonderful people and I felt they deserved to have the world know exactly how I felt about them.

If there could be more foster parents just like them than the Foster Care System would not fail our children, because the Tazelaars are exactly what a Foster Home should be.

Lawanda, treated me with so much respect and dignity, she treated me like one of her own, in fact she had a daughter who was two at the time named Jamie, whom I adored. I may have left their home under bad circumstances; however, I hope they will know that I have much respect for both of them and their family.

The definition of a foster mother and father should be that of Jim and Lawanda Tazelaar, caring, sincere, people who want to make a difference in another child's life. Not only did Jim and Lawanda welcome me into their home so did their ENTIRE FAMILY!!. I felt like I had a sense of belonging. Unfortunately, I had a sleep issue, and it caused me to talk in my sleep and say some bad things, and during one of these sleep issues, I threatened them and terrified both Lawanda and Jim. I regret having talked in my sleep, I do believe that they felt I was awake but I was not and I remember nothing of the incident. I did however read a bit about it in my social services file, and it reflected how I scared them and I truly am sorry that this occurred and If I could have ever changed this, I most certainly would.

Lawanda was one of those active moms, she would think nothing of packing up the bike with the little seat on the back, she would pack Jamie in it and off we went out the door. She was very neat and tidy, and just an all around beautiful person inside and out. Lawanda was short with short black hair and had a dark complexion. Jim on the other hand was funny had a good sense of humor but was your typical family man.

They were fantastic foster parents, although I didn't always listen to the rules in their home, I have the utmost respect for them. Like I said their entire family accepted me as if I was their own. They didn't care that I was a foster child. I guess that is what I found unique about this family and why I liked it. I finally found that I was accepted, as I was.

I don't think Lawanda liked my mother and I truly understand that if this in fact was the case I know the reasons why. For the short time Lawanda and Jim were in my life, they were more my parents than any other placement or my own biological parents had ever been. Lawanda saw firsthand at Christmas how my mom didn't want me to come and visit her, she was there to pick up the pieces when I was upset.

While living with the Tazelaars, I was taught respect, how to get ready for the real world, and responsibility but most of all I was taught that I was a good person and that I was normal. I thank both Jim and Lawanda for that. Lawanda's mom Yvonne was wonderful as well and so was her husband

Lester, god bless his soul as he's no longer here. They were all fantastic. Lawanda's sister Leona was really nice, all of their family treated me so respectfully and nice. I had my moments but really it was like I was their kid, I was not treated differently because I was in care and this was the very first time that I had been treated like a typical teenager. When I was 21 , I got married and invited the Tazelaars to my wedding. They attended and it was a blast. One thing I do remember, if Lawanda ever had a few drinks on the weekend she was so giggly and happy. It was funny, she would talk loud and laugh so hard. You could always tell when she had a few and was tipsy. She didn't do it often but it was funny.

Jamie was so cute and adorable, again my memory of her is when she was two years old however, I did have the pleasure of seeing her again at my daughters first birthday, and I don't think she remembered me.

I guess that not all foster parents are bad, as the Tazelaars were the best. No thanks to the Social Services, though. I believe Jim and Lawanda were foster parents for a reason.

When you graduate out of the foster system, you learn many things, first of all you begin to realize that society has an opinion about you growing up in care and how it is all the child's fault, at least some people feel this way.

You also begin to find yourself and realize that you don't have all the necessary skills that you need to live on your own. In foster care/group homes you are not taught on how to hold down a job, how important getting an education is, and how important it is to keep a clean house or how budgeting skills are important.

You are also not taught the social skills to handle the outside world. You truly are not aware of how to act, and how to deal with the real world as an adult. I was seventeen I had just graduated from high school, and I had just had the sleep talking incident at the Tazelaars, so it was felt that I should live on my own.

They helped me rent an apartment above "Farmer Becks", a farmers market store. I would now be on Semi-Independent Living, meaning that Lawanda would still check in with me, she took me to buy cleaning supplies second hand furniture etc. She basically showed me how to set up on my own.

Living on your own on Semi-Independent Living, is tough when your seventeen, as you will quickly learn that you will be taken advantage of if you are not careful. All of a sudden you will find that your house is a crash pad for every single neighborhood kid.

My first place was very cute, it was a one bedroom apartment located on top of a Farmers Market. You walk in and it's a huge room that is the living room, then there is the kitchen and just off of it was the bedroom. Not bad for a seventeen year olds place.

Lawanda took me to buy furniture and dishes, and other stuff but other than that I was on my own. I started attending the College of the Caribou shortly after getting my own place, as well as I was working part time still at the Denny's restaurant. The restaurant job didn't last long because I just couldn't' handle waitressing.

They call it semi-independent living because they supposedly check in on you and you have to write reports. Essentially, when I was living in Williams Lake on my own I did not even do this.

One night I found out all to well that I should really be careful as to who I have over at my house. A guy named RICK he was an old man came to my house for whatever reason I don't know. My boyfriend Bruce who was a biker was over, and for some reason or another I ended up drunk, which was really strange because I was not old enough to drink. I remember drinking this stuff that was like an orange color and it tasted like peaches.

I remember this Rick guy, coming into my room and raping me, I remember wanting to move but I couldn't move, I remember Bruce coming in and him thinking I was cheating on him but I wasn't . This guy was raping me and no one did anything about it. He took off after he was done with me and went and got into the purple dented truck. I called 911 but the police just came and got him for impaired, I don't think they believed me that he raped me. Once again here I was a minor and no one believed me that I was being sexually assaulted.

I had to drop out of college after this ordeal as I ended up with a very bad case of some sort of disease where my mouth was puffed out, I couldn't go anywhere I was too embarrassed. This led to my failure at college. I decided to take off and move back to Prince George.

Shortly before I turned nineteen, I made the decision to relocate back to Prince George, because I wanted to be closer to my family. I found a cute little basement suite on Quince Street, which is in the neighborhood called the "Hood", due to the seedy people that would hang out there, I myself had no issues. During this time I started working at a variety of fast food chains. One in particular I liked was McDonalds. I was still receiving money from Social Services because I had not aged out of care yet. I would meet with the mentor person once a month at which time it was required to give them a budget and that kind of thing. I enrolled at the College of New Caledonia in a legal secretary program but dropped out shortly after as I was not sure what I really wanted to do. I knew I wanted to work, and have a good job but I just didn't have the education behind me to obtain this. After about a year I decided I wanted to live in an apartment, so I moved into one in the heart of town. It was shortly after I moved into the apartment that I met a guy who was very cute, and he just so happened to be my letter carrier.

That was when I met Dave. Dave was my first true love. Yes I can actually say it. I loved Dave, I wanted to marry him have kids with him, and be with him forever. However, it didn't work out that way at all.

Dave was quite a bit older than me and he didn't like the fact that I was nineteen. He was thirty six , and of course I was nineteen. He was so cute. It was at this time that my mom had decided to move back from Ontario, with my step father and his two kids, and they needed a place to stay.

Dave was so helpful he leant me all these rollaway cots so that my mom and my stepfather and his two kids, could have something to sleep on when they all of a sudden decided to move back to BC from Dryden Ontario. I allowed them to spend a month with me in a bachelor suite that I was renting.

Dave was handsome, and I took quite the fancy to him. I fell in love with him. I spent time at his house regularly. My mom met him and also liked him. Dave was just the type of guy that when you were sick he brought you chicken soup, and a whole wack of over the counter medicine to help you get better.

He was my guardian angel. That is of course until I found out he had skeletons in his closet. I went over to his house, and the first thing that didn't hit off with me was he had a dog named bandit. I was terrified of dogs, the second thing was Dave was pot & coke head. He would smoke pot, and do coke on weekends, and thus is the way I was introduced to it.

The very first time I tried cocaine, with Dave, I felt funny, my lips went numb and all of a sudden I had tons of energy. But then my heart started to race and I felt like I was going to pass out. I did cocaine with Dave, for about a year usually on the weekends only , I didn't do it every weekend just every odd weekend.

For some reason Dave and I had a falling out which led to me deciding to move to Vancouver. I was tired of Prince George, and I was tired of living in a bachelor suite going nowhere.

Dave was nice and moved me to Vancouver. It was at that time we broke up shortly after Labor Day Weekend as he had chosen to go river rafting with a woman named Angela. It worked out for them I guess because they ended up getting married and having kids. The funny thing was he always told me he didn't want children. My mother told him I poked holes in a condom to try to get pregnant but that was totally not true, but that's what broke up our relationship. I graduated out of care in April 1994 when I turned 19.

Chapter 12 "The Addict in Me"

I had made the huge decision of relocating myself back to Vancouver, after all part of my childhood was spent in the Vancouver city. I was a city girl.

I had decided for whatever reason to answer an advertisement in the Vancouver Province Newspaper for a roommate wanted ad. I called the number in the ad to find a man answer the phone. When I told him I was a single woman looking for a place to rent, he informed me he rented the main floor of a house with his son, and that they have a room to rent. After finding out they were paramedics and lifeguards, I decided to rent it.

Living with Paul, and Wolfgang, at first was okay. That was until unfortunately I had gotten tied up with some people that perhaps I should never had. My daily routine was to go to the Muffin Break restaurant up the street on Kingsway and Joyce, and have coffee and tea with a couple that were regulars there. For the most part now things were okay. I met an individual named Fazil, who was of a different origin, he introduce me to the Vancouver drug scene by giving me cocaine. Unfortunately I was very naïve as I was still very young as I was only 19, and I did cocaine with him. I remember going to his house hanging out in his bedroom he had this very large bed, at which time I would sit on it and watch him roll in rolling papers marijuana and cocaine. We smoked it, we also snorted it. It was at this time that I was raped at gun point by him. I remember being terrified wondering what was going to kill me first the cocaine or this guy whom I had recklessly got involved with although I didn't know him.

This of course is what you need to be careful when you are in a big city like Vancouver, and you are young and stupid like I was. I remember walking home feeling very violated, it felt as if every step I took I was going to die or pass out. I remember reaching my house and I went home. Paul was inside and I went up to him and told him what I had done and that I thought that I had overdosed or something, because I had started hallucinating and shit and I felt like everything was closing in on me. I also felt that I was going to have my heart pound right out of my chest. He tested my vitals and told me I needed to get to the hospital but that I couldn't call from the house because of what he did for work , and because he smoked pot.

I remember walking down the street and again every step I took felt like I was walking on air but my legs were having a hard time taking me to where I wanted to go as I was so high. I remember walking into a Chevron gas station, and I remember asking them to call 911. I remember sitting on the floor waiting for an ambulance which eventually arrived.

When the ambulance attended, I remember feeling embarrassed, as I was not your typical drug addict, yes I had used drugs on and off for an extended period of time however, I was not an addict, hell I didn't have needles in my arms, and I didn't have to have my drugs, to fit in to socialize. The ambulance attendant took me to the hospital where I spent the next 3 months. They called my dad, who was my only relative in Vancouver, whom actually came to visit me. This really scared me because my dad, HATED hospitals, and he came to the hospital to visit me. I remember the conversation he had with me that day, as if it was yesterday. My dad said that I was stupid to have tried drugs from someone I didn't know and that I should have come to him if I wanted to try it because then he would have showed me what each and everything was if I was adamant of doing it. He never really told me not to do them just that I should do it with him because then I would be safe. I ended up staying with my dad for a couple days after that until I was back on my feet again. I have never touched drugs since that day because of the feelings I had gotten. I scared myself straight especially when the curtains felt like they were closing in on me. It was very scary. Why people do drugs is beyond me.

I guess doing drugs for me was an escape, it was hey look at me I fit in with you because I'm high. This wasn't the only time I had ever used drugs. The very first time I tried drugs, was when I dropped acid when I was 18. I dropped it with my sister of course, I remember I did half a dub (square), I took this at 11 PM thinking it wasn't doing anything I took the rest of it an hour later. Then all of a sudden I was high as kite, all I saw was colors, it was a very interesting ordeal, PLEASE DON'T TAKE THIS AS ITS OKAY TO DO ACID BECAUSE DRUGS ARE NOT OKAY!!!. The first time I did acid it was amazing. My sister on the other hand hated it when we dropped she spent the entire time in the bathroom with excruciating stomach cramps and pains and felt like she was going to die. My sister did not have any fun at all. It was crazy. My sister and I did have a fun time that night. However, it was also the last time we ever did drugs together.

My drug use although it was limited I still had to deal with the affects of what it did to me. Drugs ruined my life. Although I was never paying for my drugs, I ended up finding myself surrounded by unhealthy people. I would end up with my possessions stolen, I would end up being sexually assaulted because of being under the influence, I would end up in dangerous situations. It was really bad. My rock bottom was when I overdosed, and I can honestly say unless that had happened to me chances are I would still be out there using.

I had been a frequent customer at this corner store where I met a guy named Fazel. He was a guy that was a little older than myself. He offered me to go to his house to smoke. I assumed he was talking about smoking rolled tobacco. I was wrong. We arrived at his house which was about $\frac{1}{2}$ a block away from my house. He lived in the Killarney CO-OP. We went into his house, and sat in this bedroom. At which time he introduced me to smoking cocaine. Smoking it and snorting it is what we did for the next hour or so. All of a sudden I started feeling my face go numb and my heart started to feel as if it was racing out of my chest. I started getting scared, and the more scared I got the faster my heart seemed to race.

Fazel pulled out a gun from under the bed and told me that I was going to have sex with him. I freaked. I complied not knowing what to do with this crazy guy who was pointing a gun at me and forcing me to have sex with him. When he was done I left still high as a kite. I walked home and as I did every step I took felt like I was going to pass out and die. I arrived home to find Paul in his room smoking pot from his bong. He was a paramedic but he did smoke pot. Anyways I told him what happened. I told him that I was going to pass out and that I thought that I had overdosed on Cocaine.

Paul took my vital signs and told me I had to go to the hospital as my heart was racing really hard. I remember before doing so I called my mom and I told her that I thought I was going to die because I had been smoking cocaine and I thought I was going to die. She didn't believe me. Shortly after this I walked to the Chevron gas station on the corner of Killarney Street & Kingsway in East Vancouver.

I remember the double glass doors, I walked into the gas station I looked at the woman behind the cash register and I said can you please call 911 as I was stupid and I think I overdosed on cocaine. They wouldn't call 911 but I did.

It felt like forever before the ambulance attendant arrived to collect me. I don't know if I truly would have died from the drugs I took that night but I can tell you this experience totally scared me straight and I have been clean and sober ever since. I can't be around drugs or alcohol.

Shortly after my overdose, I ended up moving to Kitsalano. It is community all on its own in the West end of Vancouver BC. Kitsalano is best known for its trendy shops, like Capers, and such, as well as its beach Kitsalano beach. I rented a room in a cute little basement from this girl named Silvia. She was a bubbly woman, with big bushy curly blonde hair, and she was one whom loved to drink, and loved the finer things in life. I must say I am not roommate material never have been never will be. I am not a very easy person to get along with in a living situation. Mainly because of my moods, and at the time I was a very messy person. We shared a basement suite, when you walk in the side of the house there is a door, then you walk into the living room. Silvia collected the nice stuff and a flare for decorating. Everything was color coordinated, Let's just say there was no place for my belongings. Silvia, was very sweet, unfortunately she ended up moving out on me because she didn't like me. I started dating people off of a telephone dating line shortly before I had moved in with her. I would meet my dates at the local coffee establishments. I was not looking to do anything other than find mister right. In any event, how the telephone dating works is this, you would log into their system. You would then record a temporary greeting which allows callers to listen to it and then the can leave you a private message for you to call them. You can get some pretty disgusting people on these lines, but it was the only option back then as the internet wasn't so well known as it is today.

I met some pretty scary people off of this chat line thingy, I remember shortly before moving in with Silvia, I had met a man named Kevin. This was when I was still living on Killarney Street, and it was shortly before my overdose. I had decided to meet him at Muffin Break, it was close by and not too close to my house. I also had friends that were regular coffee goers there so if there was an issue I could table hop and pretend I was with someone. I remember sitting at this one table facing towards the door, so I could see who was coming in and out. I remember this man walking in and he was wearing this trench coat type of thing, and he sits down at my table and asks me if I am Dianna. Thinking to myself do I tell the truth or do I lie. I admit that I am the person he is meeting. Now I am sitting looking at him thinking oh my goodness what I have gotten myself into. Sitting before me was this man that I thought was about forty or so, with very greasy brown hair, glasses, and he smelled like he had just poured a whole bottle of cologne on himself, also I could smell stale alcohol. It was disgusting. He opens his trench coat and pulled out a dozen red roses with half of them crumpled he hands them to me.

I felt utterly mortified and uncomfortable, that I all of a sudden noticed my old friend PHIL and his wife sitting at the table behind me and I said hey I can't date you that's my boyfriend I didn't realize he would be here. Kevin just stared at me as I removed myself from the table and went and sat at Phil's table and I whispered to Phil to play along him and his wife did. Kevin then left and went and sat in his car for three hours waiting for me to leave. I ended up calling the police on him right then and there and I explained to the police officers that I had met him on a telephone dating line, and that he was refusing to leave, and I was uncomfortable because of the fact I was worried he would follow me home. Police showed up and told him to leave. Eventually Kevin left. I hadn't heard from him in a month or so, and once I moved in with Sylvia, it became apparent that once I went back on the telephone dating line I had gotten snagged up with him again. Only somehow he had found out my new telephone number in Kitsalano. He could have looked me up in the phone book, but I don't know. He started leaving sexually explicit messages on my answering machine. It was really scary. It was also around this time that Terry Driver who was dubbed as the Abbotsford Killer, was roaming the streets of Abbotsford and there had been suggested sightings throughout the Lower Mainland.

Kevin began leaving some seriously sexually explicit messages on my answering machine. One particular message disturbed me so much I still remember it to this day " Dianna I love listening to you, I know if you could give me a chance I will do anything for you. I will give you anything you want. I like girls who like edible underwear etc etc. I notified the police about it, but the police refused to do anything claiming that I had recorded these messages of his profile on the telephone dating system which I did not. Regardless of the fact it was at this time that I completely lost faith in the Vancouver Police Department. I was also taking

Radio Broadcasting at the time that I resided in Kits, I would walk to and from school. I was terrified of this Kevin guy, and on one occasion I was convinced he had tried to run me over in his car when I had been walking home. I had memorized his plate number from previous. I was convinced he was stalking me, and on one occasion I was convinced he had tried to run me over on my walk home from school, I told the police that I had written his license plate on my hand during the time of the almost hit and run. I didn't think that the small fact of not actually seeing the license plate and that this little white lie would turn into an arrest of myself for public mischief. Detective Doug Lepard, took over the case, but he was not trying to charge Kevin he was looking to charge me, with public mischief. Public Mischief is a charge that consists of leading police into a false investigation. Too this day I claim that I am innocent of this although I was convicted of it, and it was all based on this stupid license plate number written on my hand. It was because of that little detail that they had charged me. I guess Kevin's vehicle had been involved in a suspicious vehicle fire the day before. I truly did not intend to mislead the police and I truly believe that Kevin was up to no good and was stalking me. However, the police didn't believe me. Again I blame it on the fact I grew up in the Foster Care system and Law Enforcement stereotypes individuals whom are raised in the system. Law Enforcement, also have issues when people continuously call police over things that are crimes but when the police decide to not follow through on charges. I will get into this later on.

I received 2 years of probation when I was convicted of Public Mischief, as well as I was not allowed on any telephone dating sites during the probation. Let's just say I had no issues with that considering, there are many undesirable people that are on those sites, there very well could be some really nice people whom resort to the telephone dating sites, however I unfortunately did not meet any.

When you are living an addict lifestyle you tend to end up around people that are unhealthy, even if you don't actively use, you tend to associate yourself with other addicts. Although I quit doing drugs and drinking, I still associated with people that perhaps I should not have been.

This includes my boyfriend at the time Anthony. I had moved out of my basement suite that I was renting with Silvia, and moved into an apartment building in Surrey, just beside the Surrey sky train station.

The building appeared at first to be a quiet complex and a good family neighborhood, although at the time I was still single I was in a long term relationship and decided I wanted to try to have a baby. Anthony and I met, when I was renting another basement suite in Surrey. I am unsure as to where we initially met but we ended up dating for 2 years.

Anthony was gorgeous. He had short brown hair, and he was built. Initially we would hang out at venues that helped keep us clean and sober. Although Anthony & I never used together we tended to go to sober dances and stuff together. I felt that perhaps we would eventually get married, I was wrong.

When we broke up I truly don't know what happened. I don't remember why we parted ways. I don't know if it was because we fought. I don't know if it was because he took my car without permission and I called the police. I don't know if it was because he took my cell phone and through it out the window.

I don't know if it is because I sued him for the cell phone bill and stuff truly I don't know what went wrong. For some reason or another, I blocked out everything from that period in my life.

Our relationship went sour and until this day I don't exactly know why. Shortly after our relationship ended, I met the man that I would eventually marry, Derek Holden.

Derek was 21 years my senior. He was the owner of a collection agency called Network International Credit. Derek and I met through my own company.

Little did I know my encounter and marriage would lead me to a mental breakdown and a very difficult time in my life. Little did I know that marrying someone you don't know all that well could cause years of grief. I was soon to realize this but not because someone had told me but because I would learn firsthand that perhaps you should get to know someone before taking the marital plunge.

Chapter 13 "Husband & Father Death Do us Part"

February 1996, was a fantastic month for me, I had just graduated from Radio Broadcasting school and had decided to go on a date with a client of my people locating agency called North American Tracing Services. One of my business clients, a man named Derek Holden, he was the owner of a Collection Agency based in the heart of Vancouver, and he had asked me on a date.

I had been single for awhile since the break up with Anthony, so I decided what the heck why not go on a date. Derek, seemed really nice on the phone and he drove a yellow Mustang GT, you know the ones all sported out. It was his baby. Our first date was at a Chinese restaurant, in the heart of Vancouver. We sat and ate Chinese and just talked. Derek was six foot four sandy brown hair, blue eyes, and gorgeous. He had a good sense of humor and was the life of the party so to speak.

Derek was twenty years older than me as at the time I was twenty one and he was forty one. To me back then age was just a number. I didn't care that he

loved Jimmy Hendrix and had all his records, and I jus
didn't know who Jimmy Hendrix was. I didn't care tha
he played baseball and loved to drink and I couldn'
stand baseball and I was sober and didn't drink
anymore. I also didn't care that he was a client. What
did know is we laughed together, we were spontaneous
and it seemed that he was the type of man I wanted to
marry. So we did. With only knowing each other for one
month we made the marital plunge and got married or
April 27, 1996 in Prince George British Columbia, ir
attendance was his father Wally Holden, myself and
about fifty people that I knew. On our wedding nigh
we were already arguing however, perhaps we should
have thought it through before getting married

Derek and I lived together after our wedding in a house
on West 76th which Derek rented. We went to work
every day, and he worked at the collection agency and
worked at my skip tracing agency which held office
space right beside his collection agency.

We went on our honey moon in whistler when it was of
season it was at this time that our marriage fell apart
Derek had a seizure when we were there and I wil
always remember it, it was like it was yesterday and
that someone had possessed my husband. Derek didn'
remember marrying me, in fact thinking back to tha
day he didn't remember much of that day. Regardless
of this he was ambulanced to Vancouver Genera

Hospital, and a few days later we found out he had Terminal Brain Cancer.

That's right Derek the man that I had just married was terminally ill. It was also after this that I refused to sleep in the same bed as my husband because I became scared that he would die in his sleep. I didn't know much about cancer, or death but all I had in my head was that there was no way I was going to lay next to him and wake up next to a dead body. That would scare the shit out of me.

Three weeks after my husband was diagnosed, my father was also diagnosed with cancer. Shocking but it was crazy, it was almost like god was preparing me for cancer because not only did my husband have stage four cancer (terminally ill) but my father also had cancer. Dad had lung cancer. All I felt like with this revelation was oh my god not only was I going to lose my husband, but I was going to lose my dad as well. After my dad & husbands diagnosis's I started recoiling into my own little world. I had stopped sleeping with my husband, it felt like a tug a war with providing transportation for my husband to the BC Cancer Agency, as well as for my father who also needed a ride to his cancer appointments.

The war between the time I spent with my husband and the time I spent with my dad, took a toll on my marriage. It took such a toll that one Sunday I decided to go into work, and back then I only had a pager, (there were no such thing as cell phones). I received a page from my husband, so I called home. It was when I called home that I realized our phone was disconnected. Shortly after this, I called our telephone company and I was informed my husband had cut it off deliberately. I then got a page from my husband telling me that our marriage was over and that he would leave my stuff on the curb.

I freaked out not knowing what to do , I did what I could only do I tried to commit suicide. I decided I would jump off of the Burrard Street Bridge, as it was walking distance to my office. This of course was the beginning of my mental break down. Just everything had seemed to pile up. I had nowhere to live, I didn't think that I should just walk home after all I was married to the guy. He couldn't really force me out of the house, but he had. And that was the reality. In any event, I called the Vancouver Crisis Line, this is a line that people can call when they are needing someone to listen to them. I told them what I planned to do. I then took off from my office and walked to the bridge. It was just as I got up on the bridge deck that the police picked me up and arrested me under the Mental Health Act. I was handcuffed and taken to St. Paul's hospital to be evaluated by a doctor because of what I was planning to do.

During this point in my life I wanted to die, mainly because of the fact that my husband left me, my dad had cancer and truly I felt it was the end of the road for me. I had no place to go, I had an office but how long would that last for, I had no money, my job was basically nonexistent as my husband was my financial backer. And after all it was his collection agency that was my number one client.

After the police arrested me for trying to jump off the bridge, I ended up staying at a woman's shelter, until I found a new place which I had made a poor choice to share with a woman from the Woman's Shelter named Natalie K. Now Natalie was from the country of Ziar. She was in her thirties, and spoke fluent FRENCH but no English. Her understanding of the English language was very little and I blame this on all of the issues that took place the day we moved in with each other.

We had just moved in with each other into a basement suite. We didn't have a phone yet as we had just moved in. At the time I was quite a messy person. In any event I was doing the dishes and Natalie, was mad because I had dirty dishes on the floor. She threatened to call the police because I had dirty dishes on the floor. The woman was psychotic. I was quickly doing the dishes as I was going to be heading out with a guy I had met who was a pilot. I quickly did the dishes then all of a sudden Natalie started screaming that I was going to kill her or something it was very strange. Eventually two people came in my house from nowhere and asked what was going on. I explained I had no idea what was happening I was doing dishes and my roommate started screaming saying I was going to kill her. I left to go to the payphone to call the police. I informed them that my roommate was accusing me of trying to kill her with a knife, when in fact I was doing the dishes. As I started walking back home, a police dog and a police officer was walking toward me when the dog saw me it started barking.

The police officer asked me to stop and put my hands on my head, I did as he instructed me. He then walked me over to my front lawn where a female cop showed up and tried accusing me of threatening my roommate with a knife. I tried explaining that is not what happened. The police officer came out with a butcher knife that I had washed from when I was doing the dishes. That's when I flipped out. I was being framed, I didn't do anything. This cop accused me of shit when I hadn't done anything at all but wash the dishes.

I started yelling names at her and was quite rude, she shoved her knee in my back and then yanked me up handcuffed behind my back. The police then took me to the police station, it was at this point that I completely freaked out. In my opinion if they were going to arrest me for something then it better be for something valid and for something that I actually did not just accused of.

As I was being booked into the police station, I saw my opportunity, I saw a police officer have a gun in their holster, just as I was being uncuffed, I grabbed the police officers gun, almost unholstering it, then I was physically attacked by about ten members of the police department.

I was held in custody and went to court the next day I was placed on remand which meant that I had to stay in jail until my next court date, and at this point I was also sent for a thirty day psychiatric assessment at the Forensic Psychiatric Institute. I just kept thinking to myself, why is this all happening to me. First I get married and I think that I'm going to live happily ever after only to have my husband get diagnosed with cancer, and have him kicking me out of our rental unit. Then my dad is diagnosed with cancer, and for all I know I could be stuck in this jail or psychiatric place and never get the opportunity to see my father again before he dies.

The shit that was running through my head was shocking. I was scared, and deep inside I was just a little girl who hadn't grown up yet and truly didn't understand why what was going was going on.

Staying in the Forensic Psychiatric Institute was terrifying. This was a psychiatric hospital where people who were found not criminally responsible for very serious crimes were housed away from the public. When the sheriffs van firs t drove up to the facility after my court appearance I was praying that it was all a big nightmare and that I would wake up anytime. Unfortunately this was not the case.

As the sheriffs opened up the back of the van, to let me out with my handcuffs on, I was led into this facility that looked like a horror show. I was led in through these doors, at which time I was met by some very large woman who just commanded things from me.

They all wore white, and this one woman, instructed me to take all of my clothes off and then gave me a pair of coveralls that have only Velcro on them I was taken into a room where there was a big bath tub. This woman watched me the entire time and she told me to get into the bathtub and clean up. She then forced me into these coveralls and I was left in a room with the door locked for a day or so, until I saw a psychiatrist.

It was shortly after this I was put on medication, again I wasn't psychotic I had no diagnosed psychiatric illnesses but here I was order for a psychiatric evaluation and all of a sudden put on psychiatric medication.

I was taken to see a psychiatrist in the room and he asked me the standard questions, do I see things, do I hear voices, what do I think when I watch television. Do I know the difference between what is real and what is not real. Do I think people are talking to me through the television. Why did I try to kill myself on the bridge. Did I know I was placed there for an assessment. Was I aware that no one ever gets out of there most people had been there for years, and it was up to him to decide whether or not I would get out of there. This was just really fucked up and scary all at the same time.

I was not mentally ill, nor did I have anything that these other people had. I was terrified. The scary thing was that I was drugged up and if I had to defend myself which did happen on one occasion I couldn't.

The daily routine was to sit around and smoke, that was it sit smoke and zone out, everyone in there were like zombies. No one could think for themselves, you would see people walking around aimlessly talking to themselves, or arguing with themselves, or even threatening   people.

This one woman whom I had the not so pleasure of meeting named Diana Dyke, she was placed there because she killed her husband while he was sleeping by lighting him up like a chimney by setting him and his bed on fire. She was not criminally responsible due to the fact she had a mental illness and didn't know right from wrong because of it.

One time we were sitting at the table and she was sitting there than for whatever reason she thought I had taken her pictures of her family, and were throwing them or something she also accused me of kicking her under the table again I did nothing of the sort and she just thought this I guess. She walked up to me and started choking me. She put her hands around my neck and squeezed. I couldn't breathe I thought that I was going to die. I was terrified. The staff there didn't do anything. I finally got free, and there was nothing that was ever done about this person.

It was scary in this facility; finally, the day of court arrived and just before I went off to court, the psychiatrist made a point of saying that if he could he could yank me back on a mental health warrant. Although I didn't have any mental health illnesses this scared the shit out of me. Just to think that this person has such power to decide whether or not you have to stay locked up in a facility or not.

I went to court and was unfortunately found guilty, to this day I claim my innocence. I was given two years probation and I was released from jail. It was at this time that I decided to move back to Prince George.

Shortly after I was released from custody, and just prior to me moving to Prince George again, I remembered getting a page from my mom. It was March 18, 1997, and I went to the Willingdon Church and called my mom from the Pastors office. My mom told me that my dad had passed away a few minutes ago. I was devastated. I felt how could my father go so soon. I had only seen him two days prior, and although I would never have recognized him, I know he knew I was there, after all he squeezed my hand. I loved my dad so much and when he died a part of me died as well. I know that I didn't know much about my father until after his death but he was my dad and I was very sad when he died.

Just to say a little bit about my dad, for me he was my hero. Yes he had his flaws, he was an alcoholic that never went to AA and didn't believe it. Although he never admitted his alcoholism, I believe he knew he was an alcoholic. My father was also a heavy smoker, and too this day I believe that is what caused his cancer. My father was very young when he died he was 56 years of age. My dad initially worked moving furniture, then he ended up on Welfare, as well as he was a fruit peddler. I remember how he had this old truck where he would have a variety of fruit which he would park his truck on a parking lot and sell the fruit.

I loved my dad, I just wish I had more time with him to get to know him. I remember my dad would make these tricks of hiding coins in my ears. I remember climbing on his back when we were kids. I remember how he would sit in front of the television and watch shows such as Rockford Files, Un-sub, the A-Team etc. But for me dad was dad. I loved him.

In 1998 I moved to Prince George and moved into a basement suite with my sister in the College Heights area of the city. Our Landlord was an interesting person, and I think my sister took a fancy to him as he was relatively close to our age. He had a lot in common with my sister, such as a partying lifestyle, same music likes and dislikes. Living with my sister didn't last very long as we had our differences and it didn't work out. It was at this time that I committed the ultimate sisterly betrayal. Although my sister meant the world to me I truly didn't anticipate hurting her so deeply as I had.

My sister always knew that I had a gambling addiction, she always knew that I had a habit of doing stuff that wasn't exactly right at the time however, she didn't think I would do it to her. One night when my sister was sleeping I had snuck into her purse and took out her bank card. I then proceeded with my friends to the bank machine and I deposited an empty envelope into my sisters account and I took out seven hundred dollars. At which time my sister didn't have any money.

How the scam worked and why I felt that it wouldn't hurt my sister was this.

Some banks allow you to do a deposit into the bank machine, and the bank machine does not hold the funds that are in the account (now they check your credit), anyways what happened was I deposited a check that I wrote out for Seven Hundred, I would place the check into the envelope and then the check would come back as non sufficient funds (meaning no money available to cash the check). It would then leave a negative balance in my sisters account. I was charged criminally for theft under $5000 for this offence. I had done the same thing with my own bank card but due to the amount being higher they charged me with Fraud Under $5000.00.

Needless to say by me stealing my sisters bank card it ended our roommate relationship. I ended up going to court and pleading guilty and I got an Eight month conditional sentence which meant that I had my freedom in my house however, if I messed up even just a little bit I would be placed in jail to serve the remainder of the time of eight months.

I also received two years, probation. Probation is where you have to go to a person that is called a probation officer and check in with them. Sometimes the court will place certain restrictions on you such as where you live, where you cannot go, or who you are not allowed to be around. Some people cannot consume alcohol or non-prescription drugs.

For me I was not allowed to possess a bank card, I was to complete 25 hours community service work (meaning work for free) I was also check in weekly by my probation officer. For my community hours, I had to wash the vehicles of TELUS & BC HYDRO. So each day I was picked up and taken to the lot where they were parked and I washed them.

I rented a bachelor suite on fifteen avenue in Prince George shortly after I was charged. I wanted to start making something of myself.

Chapter 14 "My family"

After going through a lot with the Social Services Agency I thought I should write a chapter about my family and about my girls. My girls are amazing.

In the summer of 2000, I met my children's father Dan, at first I thought he was amazing, but of course things do sometimes change when you actually get to know someone.

Dan was six foot four two hundred pounds, and he was of aboriginal decent. He was a very good looking man in my eyes. I will always remember the day we met.

was outside of my apartment building, laying on the grass doing my homework as I was taking a police sciences class when I saw this man on a balcony. It turned out to be Dan and he was smiling at me and yelled "Hey your Cute". I looked up and noticed him. After that it was history. We introduced ourselves. He informed me he was in town from Winnipeg and how he was just visiting his friend Kelly. I knew Kelly and his girlfriend Jen from the building.

For the next month Dan and I were unseparatable. Dan would stay at my house every night and we decided to have a baby. We felt that we were meant to be together so we planned to have a baby. This wasn't the first time I had tried to get pregnant as I had tried many times in the past but was unsuccessful. Truly I didn't think I could get pregnant this time either. I was wrong. My mom had taught me a trick. If you're serious about getting pregnant, stand on your head after you have sex, because then the sperm runs down inside you rather than immediately out. I don't know if it's true or if it works, but for me I did it and a month later I did find out I was pregnant with my first child.

During my nine month pregnancy Dan decided to head back to Winnipeg, as I didn't really want to be with him because of the amount of drinking and partying he did.

As my pregnancy progressed, my relationship with my mother became a lot stronger and she was very supportive of me becoming a mother. I was starting to get worried about being a mom, you know the normal pre-parental jitters. I was okay. I absolutely loved being pregnant. I will always remember two very scary things that happened during my pregnancy with my first daughter. The first was when I was walking home and I was about 8 months pregnant and I felt like I was going to pass out. I ended up going to the hospital I was fine. However, I was worried that no one would know that I was pregnant as I was carrying her so small. The second things was my mom and I went for Vietnamese food, and I decided to have a salad roll with peanut sauce. My temples swelled up so bad that I had to go to emergency. It was the freakiest thing, even my mother said the same thing. The nurse at the hospital saw it but by the time the doctor saw me the swelling was gone. Needless to say there was no more Vietnamese Food for me during my pregnancy. I was told it could have been a food reaction because of being pregnant.

The day I went into labor was amazing, it hurt but it was amazing. I remember waking up at about eight in the morning, and I was getting really bad pains in my back. The pains weren't going and it was continuing and I called my mom.

We decided because these pains were so close together we better head to the hospital just in case I was in labor.

Upon my arrival at the hospital, it was confirmed my labor had started but I was only three centimeters dilated (and I needed to be ten) in order to have the baby. They wanted to send me home. There was no way I was going home. I was scared to go home knowing that the baby could come any time. So I was transferred to the maternity ward until I was ready to have her. The labor pains became more intense a couple hours later. I was told that because she was my first that I could be in labor for days. They were wrong. Shortly after five pm I was getting these pains so close together that they checked me again and realized I was now 8 centimeters dilated. This is when they called the doctor.

Upon the doctors arrival they decided to break my water. They used a glove with a little hook or something on it and they broke my water. Then the pains got so intense and I felt the urge to push. This was when I was in hard labor. It was about seven in the evening, I pushed hard for about half an hour. My mom was in the delivery room with me and my labor coach was also there with me. At 7:17 pm my daughter's head came out and then the rest of her was born. At first she wasn't breathing but then took her first breath. She came out so fast that she tore me and I ended up with one hundred and sixty one stitches. Just after I had her I had to push out the placenta. This is the sack which she lived in for the previous nine months. My daughter was beautiful, she had a full head of black hair which stuck up like a Mohawk. She was amazing.

I spent five days in the hospital before I was released and I went home. At the time I was living on top of a women's shelter. A few days after being home I started feeling really sick. I was getting severe stomach cramps. I remember going to see my psychiatrist that I was seeing at the time. I was with my mom at the health unit, we went up in the elevator I went to my appointment and as I came down I started to hemorrhage. Meaning that I bled so bad I ended up in the health units bathroom. I remember my mother carrying Hayleigh in her car seat, she was still very newborn. I thought I was going to die. My mother grabbed a nurse, and they called an ambulance. I went to the hospital and they were extremely rude to me at the hospital. They kept saying there was nothing wrong with me.

I didn't believe this I knew there was something wrong. I could barely bend down, I couldn't even lift my daughter who was only about 6 pounds.

I hemorrhaged again and I went in by ambulance, and again they didn't do anything in fact they almost refused to see me. They tried telling me to stop being so scared and that there was nothing wrong. You see they saw me as a person who had mental health issues and judged me by that and just assumed there was nothing wrong. When I get scared about a health thing especially when I am bleeding so heavily I cry. I am scared. If the nurses would have just explained that everything was going to be okay then I would have been a lot calmer. But I was in a lot of pain I was getting severe cramps, I also was bleeding and I was terrified. It was more than just a period I was soaking through pads but no one would believe me.

Again I was sent home. Then Saturday came around it was about eight in the morning. I went to the bathroom and plop there was this huge clot that landed in the toilet. I was terrified, I called my friend the only person I could think of to come over and pick up Hayleigh for me and watch her so that I could go and take this thing into the hospital with me. She came over, and I went racing back to the hospital with this strange thing that came out of me. This time at the hospital I was seen by a gynecologist who tested the thing I fished out of the toilet and I was told it was placenta. In fact it was retained placenta. I was told that I had to go for an emergency DNC (operation) to clean my wound out because I had retained Placenta from the birth of my daughter. I was also told that I could die if it was left in me because it was poisoning my body. (Now they couldn't figure that out earlier on) Perhaps if the hospital would have taken me seriously instead of judging me because of my mental health issues then they would have caught it. This is one of the reasons I hate it when people stereo type people who have mental health issues.

So I remember my sister coming to visit me shortly before I went in for the surgery. It was a quick surgery and my friend watched Hayleigh at the time.

Once I had the surgery I was okay. When Hayleigh was about seven weeks old, I started getting post partum depression. What this meant for me was I was thinking very negative thoughts about hurting her or placing her somewhere so I didn't have to be a parent. I felt inadequate as a mom because she wouldn't latch. I also wasn't used to multi tasking with her. In fact I never had held a baby before I had her so I truly didn't know what to do. I was on a medication as well that made me extremely tired and it also made me clumsy. I would wake up in the middle of the night as she was feeding every two hours, I remember the first time I was so groggy that I dropped her. She wasn't hurt but it terrified me. I remember the second time I dropped her was on to the mattress in her crib. I took her to the hospital when this happened because I was a new mom and I was worried. It was at this time that social services was called on me the first time.

I blame this all on the medication that I was on at the time, and the fact that I wasn't used to multi-tasking with a baby in my arms.

Social Services checked it out and nothing developed when the people at the hospital reported me.

I continued to have post partum depression so I went to my mom for help because I figured she would know what to do. By this time Hayleigh would scream 23 out of 24 hours per day. She was a very colicky baby and I was having a very hard time dealing with it because I took it personally and felt she hated me. I didn't think babies were supposed to cry this much but she did. I told my mom what was going on.

Many nights my mother and I would go driving down the road in my mom's van with Hayleigh strapped in her car seat as it was the only way it would get her to be quiet. Thank god for my mom on those nights because I didn't have a vehicle.

Being a single parent is tough, but you do what you got to do. When Hayleigh was about nine months old she started having these apnea spells (she would stop breathing and go blue) this led to many hospital visits and eventually it led to the doctor sending her to BC Children's Hospital for further tests.

When they sent Hayleigh to BC Children's Hospital in Vancouver, BC, they sent Hayleigh to a SCAN clinic. This is a clinic that checks to see if you are abusing your children. They actually thought that I intentionally hurt my baby and I didn't. The results showed that I didn't do anything but they did find out that Hayleigh had left sided torticollis. This was when a baby takes preference over a particular side of their body. They also found out that she had a lopsided face and her left cheek was much larger than the other.

It was at this time that I contacted Dan, in Winnipeg because I was worried about our daughter. I eventually got a hold of him but he was drunk. He came down to Prince George once again and met his daughter for the very first time when she was nine months old in a Humpty's Restaurant. It was not the ideal place for a father to meet his daughter but he met her for the first time and it was magical.

Dan ended up going back to Winnipeg as he couldn't stay. I continued to struggle with parenting Hayleigh on my own. I was working at the Mr. G's store as a cashier while my mom watched Hayleigh. I remember one time coming home from work and my daughter was not with my mother. At the time my mother and I were living together because I needed the extra help with my daughter. I was a new mom and I didn't know a lot about parenting. I remember the day my mother took Hayleigh as if it was just yesterday.

It was early evening I just got off work. I walked in and Hayleigh wasn't there. My mom was sitting outside smoking and had a piece of paper in her hand and said that she had something for me. She gave me a piece of paper telling me she had an EX-PARTE order of Sole-Custody of my daughter. Meaning that I was no longer the custodial parent of my daughter that she did. I flipped.

I had reached out to my mother for help and I felt so betrayed by her when I found out she went behind my back and stole my daughter from me. I asked where she was and my mother would not tell me.

I left and called my NA sponsor and talked to her for hours. I didn't know what to do, My sponsor told me to keep it together because if I ended up in the hospital or out using drugs or drinking I would never get my daughter back. I decided to call the Ministry for Children & Families social workers, because I felt that my mother was a danger to my child. I called and made a report I told them that my mother went behind my back and got an order of sole-custody of my infant daughter, I told them that I had heard my mother calling Hayleigh "DIANNA", I have also heard my mother refer to herself to my daughter as "MOMMY", and there was a list of other stuff that I informed them of.

The social workers decided to remove my daughter from my mother's care and placed her into a foster home. They would have returned immediately to me but I needed an order of custody first. It took me two weeks to get one. Once I had the order immediately they returned her to my care. Unfortunately I agreed to a supervision order which was initially drafted by my mother. It was also at this time when my daughter was in a foster home, me and their dad got back together for a one night stand, as he was living in an apartment in town.

Once I got my order of custody back from my mother for Hayleigh I decided to move in with Dan. We rented an apartment and started parenting Hayleigh together. Shortly after we moved in together I found out I was pregnant again with my second child. This was quite a surprise as we had not planned to have a second child as we had just gotten back together.

So here I was living with the father of my daughter, pregnant for a second time, not wanting to be pregnant right at that time.

My pregnancy didn't last long, in fact neither did the relationship with my children's father. At least not the first time. Dan was a couch potato. He also had substance abuse issues, he liked to smoke pot and cigarettes as well as drink. I was the only person that had money in the house and he was not supporting himself. I smoked myself but at least I had money to pay for them.

Dan went to work tree planting in June of 2002, while he was a way I had made the decision to leave his sorry ass. Unfortunately when he came back he threatened to kill me and take Hayleigh to a reserve. (First Nations Land). Fortunately for me the police heard his threats on the phone and arrested him. Now he was charged with uttering threats. I was still pregnant with our second daughter and Dan and I got together for a few days he was upset and pushed me into a door handle, I started spotting and ended up going to the ER because of it as I was six months pregnant.

The next morning it was eight am. It was August 8, 2002. I woke up and it looked like I had peed myself. I got up to make Hayleigh French toast as usual. My mom who lived in an apartment down the hall came over and told me to sit down that she thought my water had broke. I didn't believe her. I told her I was fine. My friend Brian came and picked up Hayleigh and took her to daycare for me and then drove myself and my mother to the hospital.

At the hospital, I went immediately to LDR (Labor & Delivery) as I was six months pregnant. They did an amniotic fluid test to see if I had my water break. It was confirmed it had. They contacted the OBGYN on call which came and did an ultra sound. It didn't look good, my baby was breach (BACKWARDS) and there was NO water left in the sack. Immediate arrangements were made to air ambulance me to Vancouver to give birth to her. I needed to have a cesarean section immediately.

I remember going into the air ambulance and telling the ambulance attendants that if I had my baby on board not to let me see because I would be scared. We arrived at Royal Columbian Hospital, and I was immediately taken into the operating room. They did another ultrasound and put an epidural in my back and froze me. They then opened me up and my baby was born. I didn't know for five days what sex my baby was. In fact the whole fiasco at the hospital was a nightmare.

The hospital staff took my stress and trauma of my daughter's birth as that I was a mother on drugs which I wasn't. I didn't do drugs or even drink for that matter.

I had a nurse tell me that I was better off to leave and go back to be with my other daughter as my daughter that I had just given birth to would not even know I existed because she was too small and wasn't meant to be born yet.

I had a very difficult time breast feeding because I had no support. But there was absolutely no way that I was going to leave the hospital and leave my baby. I ended up staying at a women's transition house and I borrowed a breast pump from the Health Unit. Eventually my daughter was transferred back to Prince George.

When we arrived back to Prince George, it came to be known that the nursing staff at the hospital in

Vancouver gave the special care nursery the wrong report on the wrong baby for my daughter.

I had went and expressed my breast milk so Ciarra my newest arrival could have it. I received a message from the Chemical dependency unit telling me that they can help me get off drugs. I don't do drugs. This was strange. I was also told that my daughter had tested positive for cocaine and that she had hepatitis C again if this was true there was a serious problem as I didn't have hepatitis C nor was there any way that my daughter could have cocaine in her because I didn't do drugs period. I started questioning the fact that perhaps they sent the wrong baby up from Vancouver because it was not possible what was being said.

Fraser Health who was responsible for the admissions at Royal Columbian Hospital the hospital which was where I gave birth to my newest arrival, decided it was best to do a Maternity test. They needed to confirm the correct baby was given to me. It took six months for them to come back with the results meanwhile I had to take precautions against HEP C so that I wouldn't get infected nor would my other daughter get infected.

We also ran a private test, and it was confirmed that Ciarra did not have Hep C nor was she someone else's child. She was my own flesh and blood and it turned out to be a careless nurse from Vancouver who got her patients mixed up and gave a verbal report on another baby without having the correct chart in front of her.

This whole ordeal made it difficult for me to bond with my daughter for six months because if for example she wasn't mine I would have had to give her up while they looked for my child.

After we returned to Prince George, Hayleigh, me and Ciarra all moved in with Dan. We spent a couple years together until November of 2004 at which time I decided to break up with their father given his drug abuse and drinking issues.

It was the first of November 2004 when I got my own place I decided to rent an upstairs of a duplex. Moving into this house truly was the worst thing I could have ever done.

However, I had to leave their father because of the differences we had and because it was in the best interest of our girls to not have him around while he was under the influence of drugs and alcohol.

When Dan was sober he was an amazing father. He loved the kids, unfortunately the monkey on his back prevented him from being a dad.

I will always love my children's father and nothing will change that. I know he has a lot of bitterness about me and meeting me and the things that transpired after our break up but truly I think he loved me too. It is just unfortunate we had so many adult issues.

Chapter 15 "My Stalker & Relocation"

I had just moved into my house in November of 2004. I had just recently split up with Dan the father of my children and I was raising my two girls on my own. I was blessed because I had a really close friend named Vickie who lived right across the street from me.

Vickie was an amazing woman. She was the same age as I was. She was a plus size woman with a heart of gold. Her daughters were friends with my daughters. We shared a lot of laughs. We also were there for one another unfortunately our friendship ended years later because of miscommunication. In my heart I hope that Vickie and I will eventually make up and become friends again but I doubt that will ever happen.

Four days after moving into my duplex, I met the neighbor who lived downstairs, his name was Rick, and he was on disability through CPP because he hurt his neck during a workplace accident. Rick was about 5 foot 10 and was scrawny. He had a little grey cat and he lived alone downstairs. To my knowledge he had no girlfriend and very little friends. Rick had very thin brown hair and wore glasses, he also walked bent over because of his neck not being able to move. This was a man that would just knowing him would change my life dramatically. Shortly after moving in upstairsI had asked him if I could use his laundry facilities and he said yes. This was initially the only conversation him and I had before he decided to call me one Monday night six days after this discussion and told me that he was madly in love with me and he felt that we were supposed to be together. He was drunk. It turned out he had a major drinking problem as well as had caller id and that's how he got my number.

This should have been my first warning that something was not quite right with my neighbor. I didn't take the hint. I did however contact my landlord to inquire about him to see if he was okay. After all I was a single parent with two kids upstairs. I was told by my landlord that the tenant was okay. I was also told that Rick had been there for nine years and many tenants had issues with him in the past but I should be okay because I had children.

Shortly before Halloween time, I found a set of car keys and a bag of candy on my door with a note that states the car is mine and the candy is for the kids. My neighbor Rick had decided to buy a car at a garage sale and leave the keys for me as he felt bad that I had no vehicle. He knew I had two kids, and that I asked him for rides as I needed transportation to take the girls to daycare. Unfortunately he felt that this was my way of saying that I liked him.

We started talking and we became somewhat friends. Dan was coming over to visit the girls and it was at this time I noticed Rick change. I remember one time I didn't even know that Rick was home.

Dan came over to visit the girls and the girls then went to bed. Dan and I decided to have sex and Rick was watching us through my mail slot and you could hear him after he went downstairs get all upset. As the evening progressed, Dan for whatever reason spilled something on his pants or they got wet or something, so I decided to run them downstairs and put them in the dryer. I thought Rick had left cause his car wasn't home. I went in to the laundry room which was accessible to both my suite and Ricks suite. I then put the dryer on and put Dans pants in them. As soon as I turned the dryer on Rick came out of his suite yelling and swearing at me telling me how he should be up there with me not Dan. He had this big hate on for Dan. Rick was drunk and very scary. I ran upstairs and told Dan what was going on and then he put on my jogging pants and went downstairs. We decided to call the police because of the condition Rick was in and the threats he made towards me that night. The police showed up but couldn't do anything because Rick refused to answer his door to them.

A few days after this incident, I had one of Jehovah's Witnesses show up at my door, and she told me that she saw that Rick had a calendar with it marked down when Dan was visiting and when he wasn't he even had the times written down as to when I was on my period, she wanted to let me know cause my neighbor was creeping her out.

This was my second warning that something was not quite right with my neighbor Rick but again I ignored it and still talked to Rick when Dan wasn't around. I wasn't interested in having a relationship with him I was just interested in talking to someone because being alone was horrible. To top things off not only was I living all by myself with the girls I was still having horrendous panic attacks and I didn't like being by myself. I wasn't used to living on my own. Afterall for the first little while after my eldest was born, I lived with my mom then after that I lived with her dad. Then all of a sudden I was a single parent by myself. It seemed very lonely. It was also very scary.

Rick and I decided to open up a business and this was supposed to be something to get me off of disability. So we opened up a company called People Locaters Canada. We got ahead of ourselves and hired fifteen people, at first things were going okay except we didn't have enough business nor money coming in to pay anyone.

Rick would bargain with me, and say if I slept with him he would pay the payroll but if I didn't than there would be a lot of unhappy people. I agreed so these employees would get paid. I knew some of them had families and they really needed to get their paycheck.

Our company was a people locating agency, and our job was to track down people who had debts and turn them in for collections. Problem was we didn't have enough clientele to keep afloat. The company lasted until June of 2006 at which time I refused to sleep with Rick to get him to pay the payroll. I didn't want to have sex with him he was disgusting and I was not into a relationship with him. I did what I had to do get people paid it happened on one occasion but it wasn't going to happen again.

The end of June 2006 all of our employees walked out on us because they were two weeks behind on a paycheck and we had no money coming in. It was at this time that Rick started to stalk me and follow me in his car. It began with me moving to a house on Regents Crescent because I got into subsidized housing. I was able to rent a beautiful house and only pay Four Hundred and four dollars for rent. It was amazing. I had a big back yard, and it was beautiful. Unfortunately,

Rick was following me and he would park his car outside my house and just watch me.

It was also at this time that I had a run in with my ex-boyfriend Wayne Gauthier the one that hijacked the school bus remember him. Well I was sitting in my living room and unpacking my books and putting them on my book case when this guy with blonde hair in a poney tail and tattoos all over his arms came walking in my front door and said hey Dianna. I looked up and I didn't recognize the guy that was standing there I said yes. He said do you remember me its me Wayne you know Wayne Gauthier. I was terrified. I was flabbergasted that Wayne was standing in my doorway looking at me and I was thinking oh my god he's going to kill me. I was wrong he just wanted to tell me he was sorry and that was it he left and went back to wherever he came from (turned out he lived in the apartment building up the street from me.).

Rick continued to stalk me and it got to the point where I had to call the police and he was charged with Criminal Harassment. I ended up having to relocate to Aldergrove BC to get away from Rick. He was obsessed with me. Unfortunately, shortly after my move my children's father and Rick became hang out buddies, and what happened next was very surprising. Rick & Dan got into a fight when they were drunk, and Dan broke Rick's neck, which led to Rick being a

quadaplegic and Dan being charged with Aggravated
Assault. Here is an article courtesy of the Prince
George Citizen Newspaper talking about me testifying
at his hearing.

Ex-girlfriend testifies at trial
Written by Citizen Staff
Thursday, 22 May 2008

*The trial for Danton Lamonte Chaboyer, 34, charged with
aggravated assault, was adjourned Wednesday until June 4 to
fix a date for continuation.*
*As the proceedings resumed Wednesday morning, the Crown
called as a witness the ex-girlfriend of both the accused and
Richard David McArthur, 42, the man paralyzed after an
altercation June 3, 2007, near Esther's Inn from which the
charge arose.*
Dianna Holden, 34, now a resident of the Lower Mainland,
*said she was with Chaboyer from 2001 through Nov. 1,
2004, and there were two children from the relationship.*
*After the relationship with Chaboyer broke off with
Chaboyer, McArthur was just a neighbour at first at her
house in the central part of the city. But then they were
closer between November 2004 and Oct. 2005, although she
said she would not describe their relationship as quite to the
level of boyfriend-girlfriend. They joined in a business
venture, but that went sour and there was a court judgement
in McArthur's favour, she said. Later she made a complaint
about McArthur concerning stalking and harassment, court
heard.*
*Holden told Crown counsel Chaboyer called her on June 3,
2007, between 5:30 and 5:45 p.m. "He said he'd got into an*

altercation with Richard McArthur and broken his neck" at the level of the C6/C7 vertebrae, Holden said.

Holden said her mother monitored part of the telephone conversation.

"He said they got into a fight at Esther's Inn and he'd put him in a chokehold," she said. "He said he did it on purpose." She went on to say, "He was wanting me back because he'd done away with Richard."

Holden said Chaboyer also contacted her more recently to try to persuade her not to testify in the trial.

Defence counsel Keith Jones questioned Holden closely.

"You have an imagination," he said. "You fabricated all that to make yourself look important, didn't you?"

"That's not true," Holden firmly responded.

Jones said Chaboyer had called only about seeing the children. "You're lying," he told Holden.

"No, I'm not," she said.

The next Crown witness, Prince George Const. Bayani Cruz, said he arrived at the scene of the altercation June 3 at 1:35 p.m. and McArthur was in a vehicle.

At that point Chaboyer was trying to wake McArthur up by calling out his name, Const. Cruz said.

"He said his friend was very drunk, and his friend tried to fight him but he didn't fight back because he was very intoxicated," the officer said.

"I asked Mr. Chaboyer if he (McArthur) was OK," Const. Cruz continued. "There was no response. He was just breathing and there was some moaning."

A few minutes later, when Const. Cruz asked a fellow constable to arrest Chaboyer for assault, Chaboyer became verbally abusive with him

"He was very aggressive and very angry in a threatening

manner -- verbally combative," Const. Cruz.
After the morning break in court proceedings, the Crown and
defence agreed there should be an adjournment in the trial
to allow typed transcripts to be provided for an expected
medical expert witness to analyze along with medical
evidence. Then such a witness could offer expert testimony
about injuries sustained during the June 3 altercation and be
cross-examined, court heard. Prince George provincial court
judge Michael Gray granted the adjournment, which the
judicial case manager later set for June 4.

Due to Dan telling me that he did it on purpose to Rick it made me a witness to it and I ended up having to testify against Dan. A very awkward situation, needless to say. Dan was found guilty and was sentenced to three years in federal jail.

After Dan's trial he pretty much blamed me for his incarceration. Although it had absolutely nothing to do with me or my testimony. I cannot control how people feel and or what they think. Dan received three years in the federal penitentiary for what he did to Rick. Personally speaking I don't think he should have spent any time in custody. They both were addicted to drugs, and got into a fight. From the evidence that was stated

Rick hit Dan first so why should he end up in jail for so long.

As your reading this book you are probably thinking okay this woman is all over the map. Well I kind of was, I wrote this book in many stages and sometimes I wanted to include certain things and other times I did not. So if it seems as though you are reading that things have not exactly followed a particular order it's because truly I didn't follow a particular order.

Chapter 16 "My Mental Breakdown"

When I set out to write "Daughter's Choice", my goal was to ensure that all parties were represented equally with respect to issues that surround the failing child protection system overseen in British Columbia by the Ministry for Children & Families. My intentions were to provide a voice to the issues that are relevant to the Child Protection System as a whole. I didn't want it to be about how bad the system is but how as individuals in society can put our heads together to advocate awareness, which leads to change.

This chapter is dedicated to discussing issues within the child protection system. Growing up in foster care is scary for any child, especially when that child is scared because they are placed in a home where there are new adults whom they don't know. For some children not only the Foster Parents are new but sometimes the family have other children that are in the home which are also unfamiliar to the foster child. Foster Homes are designed with the sole purpose of keeping the child safe.

Although the Child Protection System is set up to protect children, it sometimes fails children by leaving children in Abusive homes, as well as taking children from families where no abuse is taking place.

Initially when I began the journey of this book, I was gratefully able to not include my own story of my children being apprehended but unfortunately shortly before publication, my children were apprehended based on false allegations.

It is very scary to feel how a mother or father feels when they have their children removed from their home. It is unthinkable. In my situation I had returned from a camping trip with some neighbors. You see I resided in a low income housing complex, and when you do something to piss someone off, they all gang up on you. I was very vigilant when it came to child protection matters. Unfortunately, I couldn't keep my mouth shut when I saw children being abused, & neglected.

During the camping trip I went on, my neighbors step daughter informed me that she was being touched in bad places. I immediately returned home that evening, with my girls, and contacted the Ministry regarding what the child told me the next day.

Prior to reporting what happened on the camping trip, I posted a message on the social networking site Facebook and this is what I posted:

Dianna Holden: Back at campsite just counting the hours still until I go home friends/neighbors are wonderful just sick of Campin it's not for me.

June 26 5:55 PM

Karen : Quit your complaining ···. Think of the kids ···. LOL··· June 26 8:46 PM

Dianna Holden : Im back home what a fucking nightmare that was neighbors kid disclosed that step daddy was doin something inappropriate. I freaked and came home! Thank god Im home. Now do I call social services or do I keep my mouth shut after all the mom said that her daughter lies. Perhaps she does. He seems really nice, a little bit controlling but oh well some people are like that ☺ he is very active with the kids. I'm home now little pissed that after I told the mom what her daughter said she confronted her right in front of him. Leaving the ten year old in an awkward position. June 26 11:17 PM

I'm just going to leave it because I know in my heart of hearts I don't believe he does it and if so then she should tell a teacher or someone else. June 26 11:18 pm

Karen: This is not the place for this stuff but do report what was disclosed. June 27 10:17 am.

Dianna: Do I Or do I leave it. Mom If I report it than they'll know that it was me reporting also, what if the mom is right and the kid is doing it for attention then it puts step daddy in an awkward situation.

Leanne: That should be a private message NOT a posted message. That a very awkward situation some kids have accused people of the wrong things just like my ex and his step daughter!!! Her mother got her to LIE and it was prove in a COURT OF LAW but that said my ex life was ruined except for the people who truly knew him. Lost his house his job his life pretty shitty eh so be careful what you say or do not attacking you just advising. June 27 1:22 pm

Dianna Holden: @Leanne Point taken that some kids make false allegations in your situation it was an ex that pulled that in this situation it wasn't an ex we were on a camping trip and the eldest made a bold statement I confronted the mother on it and she confronted the child in front of the alleged abuser which she should never have done. In front of him as to whether or not what the child said is true. Or not it's the mothers responsibility to deal with it. But in this particular case she chose to side with the step dad automatically. She even emailed me saying she can't live without him. Then started shit between you and I claiming I called you a crack head. You stated in pm to me so obviously there may be some validity to what the childs claiming. Why would adults bring neighbors into an issue that isn't there's. Obviously they are trying to cause shit in the complex regarding me. Why because I stuck up for her daughter. Perhaps I should have just called social services in the first place an dnot tell the mother what happened. June 27 2:34 pm

I never once mentioned your name Desiree so I am removing your comment because if it identifies you it identifies your daughter furthermore, I never said shit about Leanne but you can claime that. I make it an issue that's fine I was told what I was told by your daughter. And I took it to you and you confronted her in front of him. Simple as that . I notified social services because I had to. I don't hide behind anonymity. And I didn't do it behind your back. You brought Leanne into this by lying about me simple as that go figure.

Desiree yes you did furthermore I didn't get involved with anyone else in here (complex) I told you what your daughter said. You had the right to know. I never named you in any of these posts. As I didn't want to identify your daughter as she has the right to anonymity. Again deleting your posts. June 27 3:16 pm

Furthermore she sat on the lawn saying she was clean. Not once did I call her what you claimed I did. I lel hot it is did I call social services about this YES I had too. I don't lie about shit people may not like me because I keep to myself but oh well your making it out to be more than it is. Be an adult and quit gossiping. I told you what needed to be told that was it. I reported it cause I had to there done. June 27, at 3:18 pm

Doesn't give her the right to threaten me in front of my children either. I never did nothing to her. She had Ciarra crying because of what she was doing and saying this has nothing to do with Leanne.

Desiree: Dianna I just got off with police I am asked to ask you to stop contacting me and talking about me and my children. Everything will be logged if it continues charges will be pressed thank you.

Dianna: I have no intentions of talking to you desiree, you brought Leanne into stuff. I told you last night about the issue at hand you chose to identify yourself on FB I did not identify you at all I am not discussing it I contacted the appropriate people about what was said to me. They can deal with it I don't appreciate you bringing the neighbor into this. That has nothing to do with it and have her threatening to hurt me and wreck my van with or without my children present. This was an issue that needed to stay between us I told you about what was said. You chose to side with the individual involved I told Social Serviecs what was told to me now it is up to them to investigate it They are trained in investigations you can claim that I am lying but that's okay they will find out what they need to find out it is out of my hands do not contact me either anymore. June 27 3:37 pm

Leanne: #1you did mention her name I copied on Facebook. You continuously making yourself look like a fucken fool because people can put your lies together eventually you voicing your fuckin opinion and accusations on this wall to me would be an embaressment to 1 myself my friends and family and further more this complex you have across to everyone as were all linking up through these past weeks putting our stories together and the fucking sorry for swearing on the wall lies and problems that you have alone never mind the ones you seem to make up in your head and think that they are actually thte truth you need to seek mental health help you verbally and mentally abuse your children and many people walking by have hear d it that's a fact jack I have everything copied that you have sent me through facebook. I show that said stay the fuck away from my family or I will see you in court for the awful things you have said about me to people in the complex. Like you have continuously involved yourself in their lives piss off and get a fuckin life. You obviously have some underlying issues from your past family member or something I think you level 5 bi-polar you seriously need to call them heres the number 6048707800 you seriously need to be assessed with your outbursts one minute your happy and the next you are this revengeful hating selfish person. June 27 4:53 pm

(PLEASE NOTE ANY SPELLING ERRORS IN THESE POSTS ARE INTENTIONAL, AS I DID NOT EDIT THE FACEBOOK POSTS.)

DIANNA: Leanne, you threatened me. You had no business threatening me Desiree knew you did drugs because you said you were clean sittin on the grass of her place. Who cares this has nothing to do with you. Your looking for a fight leave me alone do not contact me again Do not call me do not show up at my house leave me and my girls alone. I never named her I know exactly what I posted this is not your issue. June 27 5:31 pm

LEANNE: By the way there was no ambulance called to the husky. Oops another lie. This one caught on tape and facebook. Oops a paper trial nice your just drowning yourself aren't you don't you know when to qqqquuuuiiiitttt. You know what lasy you don't know what were all going through in this complex get your girlfriend help she seriously needs it. And by the way how could I have possibly known about your trip when I didn't even know Des or really you just that you gossip to everyone and call the Ministry on everyone at least 6 families in here and everyone is fed up with your crap you are seriously shit disturber and you have your no called friends believing you you need help call the crisis line.

June 27 7:23 PM

DIANNA: Leanne If I believe a child is in danger its an obligation to call. I didn't want to call they are my immediate neighbors Do you think I like this no I don't then you show up at my house and threaten to beat me up ands care my children threatening to damage my van, threatening to beat me up and to call the social workers. Go ahead I had to call given the circumstances that took place. Even if I had called anonymously they would still know it was me. I don't do it behind peoples backs. I approached the mom first. It was obviously that I should not have done that and just called in why did you threaten me. What did I do to you ? Nothing We barely talk. The last communication we had was you getting cream for me and I bought you smokes. Other than that I had asked if you wanted to watch my dog prior to me going camping then you started threatening to hurt me that's why I called the police because you threatened me it was uncalled for its not like I have ever done anything to you we don't even know each other. June 27 6:31 pm

Leanne: Cause all this came to my attention today. If you really want to know. And as far as witnesses 5 people wre standing outside and I never threatened to hit her I said she verbally and mentally abuses her kids she calls them dummies, stupid people hear things through the wall. Do you live here Come to the meeting that is going to be put together by BC HOUSING that we have just asked for then you'll hear it for yourself. And see the written complaints in Diannas handwriting and the calls to BC housing now that's a paper trail can't hide the truth you'll see for yourself and then you'll be wearing egg I have everything copied that she said to me would you like to read it then maybe you'll have some compassion for what were actually being pulled into and put through when the Ministry and BC housing is being lied to. Oh what about the disease Manchowsen buy proxy maybe you have that Dianne definitely bipolar get checked. June 27 7:20 pm I never said anything about damaging your van What I said was I was going to take you to court for defimation of character and I would report you to the Ministry for abusing your kids mentally and verbally can't hide the truth It will all come out lies can't be remembererd can they you'll slip up like whats happening now. JUNE 27 7:23 PM

Leanne, you told me that you were going to beat me up. You told me I better close my door , you said that you would make sure I lose EVERYTHING my van, my kids everything since when is this your issue.? Its not so you used to do drugs big deal. Your clean so whats the issue? You started shit my children heard you you scared us, Like I said PLEASE leave me alone. I don't abuse my kids but whatever I wrote a complaint yes I did that is my right to do so simple as that again this had nothing to do with you you came up to my door yelling at me telling me that I called you a crackhead that you received a call etc. etc. I never said this then you started threatening to beat me up and damage my van yelling at me calling me names and scaring my children. This had nothing to do with you stay out of this and leave us alone. June 27 7:30 PM

As you can see from the posts this Leanne woman has some serious issues with me and sticking her nose into things that don't belong. Regardless of the fact Leanne really needed to get help because of what she did was not okay and it is not normal. To this day I absolutely hate Leanne, I wish that one day she will fall off the face of the earth, only because of the fact she made false allegations to child protection about me and I lost my children because of her false allegations.

This would turn out to be the biggest mistake of my life, because once I had reported it, all hell broke loose in the complex. A neighbor whom I will call "Leanne", who had a habit of telling everyone she was an ex-crack head, decided to stick her nose into a situation where it didn't belong. She started to threaten me, claiming that she was going to get my kids taken away and that she would call the Ministry as many times as it takes in order to get them removed. I never believed that it was possible, but on Wednesday June 30, 2010 it became a reality.

I tried to take every avenue to prevent the removal of my children prior to it taking place. I truly didn't believe it was possible that just a couple shit disturbers could call an agency that is supposed to be trained in child protection and based on malicious lies have my children taken away from me. I was wrong. DEAD WRONG! It was Wednesday morning, and it had been three days since I made the child protection complaint regarding the neighbors. I had decided to take my girls to watch the movie Eclipse, as they had been dying to see it. I will never forget everything I did that fateful morning. I provided a ride to my neighbor and her sons to go pick up her car at the local shopping mall as her husband was at work. I then stopped at the movie theater and picked up tickets for the show a

1:15 pm, not exactly in that order of course. I then returned home to feed girls lunch, it was a grilled cheese for my oldest and it was peanut butter and jelly for my youngest. We then packed into my van seatbelts and all, and just as I was pulling out, my neighbor started screaming at me that my children would be going into foster care that day. I told my children to ignore the neighbor. We then went to the show.

After the show I remember thinking that I wasn't planning on going directly home, in fact the only reason I chose to go home right after the show is I had to take my puppy Lilly out to go to the bathroom. As we pulled into the driveway I remember my eldest daughter telling me "Mom, we're going to a foster home today", I looked at her and said "No you're not". Little did I know that my daughter was right.

We pulled into the parking lot and I parked my van in my usual assigned parking spot. The girls undid their seatbelts and climbed out of the van. We walked up to the door and the girls were on the left of my door while I started to unlock the door, and it was then it happened.

Two women got out of a van and the one said "Dianna", I turned around and said Yes? The two ladies walked up to me, and the one walked right in between me and stated that she was removing my children. No explanation no nothing, and I was like WHAT! Why?

The woman replied that she wasn't going to tell me there, and thrust a card in my hand. Then without a blink of the eye, my life walked away from me with two women whom I didn't know and neither did my girls.

There was no freaking out, there was no yelling, there was no screaming, there was no oh my god my children were just taken, there was just complete utter silence of shock on my face as I closed my door.

Standing inside my house for a minute or so in complete shock, knowing what exactly had just taken place, thinking what the fuck just happened.

I picked up the phone on the counter, and all of a sudden I was like okay I know their gone but why? I called my support worker Maureen who came into my house on a regular basis, and informed her of what had just occurred, she was flabbergasted. I then hung up and called the social worker office, and they didn't know why the children were taken, just that they were claiming that I neglected my children and that I was unable or unwilling to parent them. Thinking to myself that this would soon be straightened out and that it is completely obvious they didn't have the whole story I waited for the social worker to call me.

At six thirty pm I received this call, at which time I explain the threats the neighbors made, I explain the camping trip, I explain the bullshit that occurred with the neighbors and how they did this in retaliation against me based on my complaint I made on the neighbor. They told me they took my children because of Yelling & Swearing, they claimed they were not wearing seatbelts, they claimed they were at the park at night, they claimed that they were left home alone etc. All of which was complete and utterly false. My children were nine and seven at the time.

The next day was Canada Day which was a national holiday therefore, nothing could be done. I was asked to go to the social workers office on Friday to meet the social workers, which I agreed to.

As Friday came, I knew I needed to have a witness with me at the meeting with the Social Workers, not only to ensure that I remain calm as I was hopping mad but to ensure that my words are not twisted. I brought a neighbor who had witnessed the "Leanne", woman threaten to make false complaints about me. Walking into the meeting at the Aboriginal Social Services Office, I truly believed that they would hear what I had to say, that they would realize that the complaints that were made were false, and that they would return my girls to me. This was not the case. After all agencies like this one were all to quick to remove children from a loving environment, based on hear say.

We arrived at the office at ten am. I had decided that I wouldn't eat breakfast prior to attending because

I figured I would only be there for a few minutes. I had packed two back packs full of stuff for my girls so that they would have some of the comforts from home. My neighbor whom I'll call "Tina", came into the meeting with me. We were shown the way to the board room.

Upon entering the board room we sat down at an extremely oversize table. My neighbor "Tina", sat on my left with her infant child, and then there were the two social workers on my left.

The one social worker introduced herself as Maggie, and the other one a much older lady was Linda. Maggie was the social worker whom had attended my residence and took my children.

So we started talking and Social Worker Maggie, did all the talking while Linda did the writing and took notes. What happened next was unbelievable, I was interrogated for five hours straight, I stopped on one occasion to go to the bathroom. During the course of the five hours, I was asked about every aspect of my life, both my childhood, and then of course every moment every allegation everything that was ever mentioned regarding my daughter since the year 2001 when she was born.

I was told they were concerned that I had a fascination with Pedophilia, (thus because I wrote the book "Convicted of Abduction & Murder Online, Based on the Victoria Stafford Case", and they claimed a man whom I had been in contact with William Murtough was a convicted pedophile in the United States, which he most definitely WAS NOT one. They made these horrifying allegations, that they had no evidence to back up. I was accused of allowing my children to sneak out a bedroom window which was at least 20 feet from the ground. I was accused of allowing my children (9 & 7 years old) to stay at the park at 1:30 am – 2:30 am. I was accused of leaving them home alone for days at a time. (My eldest I had left home for little 15 minute increments) as she was learning responsibility and I was told that it was okay.

I was told that I hit my daughter, I was told that I yelled and sweared at my daughter (the yelling and swearing was about the only truth to the entire complaints).

They told me they felt that I was emotionally unstable to raise my children. It was a very frustrating five hour interrogation and by the time it was over I was exhausted. I realized oh my god they are not going to give my children back. I went out to my friends car gave the social worker the bags, and I wrote a note telling my girls how much I loved them. That was it. No Access, no nothing.

The social workers at the time of Friday's meeting didn't even provide paperwork to tell me specifically what they were accusing me of. It's one thing to say that you are abusing your children but maybe they should be specific. I do know during the removal they were unaware that I had professionals coming into my home. They did not know that I had the Child & Youth Mental Health worker in to see my eldest, they did not know that I worked with a woman who helped me deal with my panic attacks. They also did not know the girls were in licensed daycare. For an agency to believe that children were in danger, why wouldn't' they look into what the parents are claiming prior to removal? My children were never in any danger, after all we had just returned from watching a movie.

Tuesday, rolled around, and this was time for court. Hoping that I would actually be able to talk to a judge and tell them exactly what happened. I wanted to tell the judge that the whole entire reason that I was going through this hellish ordeal was because I made a child protection complaint on my neighbor and that he retaliated by getting four people whom look like they have no connections to each other to call in complaints in a short period of time. I wanted to tell the judge that "Hey these social workers came to my door as I was returning from a movie with my girls and gave me no explanation for why they were taking my children." I wanted to scream hey Judge, there has been a huge mistake here.

You see I got the paperwork the morning of court and it specifically showed that there were 3 complaints made on the 28, and the 29 of June, and then they showed one complaint on the 15 of March allegedly. This occurred after the call I made to Child Protection Services about the neighbor. It also happened after they arrived at my house in March, which reflected a false complaint. They claim that the same complaints are made over and over again, however what's the easiest thing to say when making up malicious lies about someone to child protection workers um she yells and swears at the kids and calls them names, or they are left home alone, or they get hit.   These are typical complaints anyone could make about someone, and they are also very common child abuse complaints so of course they would be continuously the same complaints over again.

Court commenced at 9:30 am, finding my lawyer was a daunting task, but once I found her I wish I hadn't. The lawyer whom I had spoken with briefly the day before, who was swearing and you could hear her taking a deep drag of a cigarette during our telephone conversation was sitting on a bench. I walked up and shook her hand with a firm handshake and sat down beside her. She was a short chubby lady with very thinning hair almost bald, grayish color. Just as I leaned over it hit me, the overwhelming smell of Alcohol mixed with tobacco smoke. The pungent smell almost made me vomit. I looked at her, and I noticed that her eyes were red and glassy, I also noticed that when she talked her speech was slurred and her breathing was rapid. I excused myself from the bench and walked into an office that had the name tag Legal Aid on the door and walked in where I found a woman in a nice suit standing beside the desk. I informed her that I needed a lawyer as the one I had was drunk.

The woman asked who it was that I had and I told her who it was, she stated that I would need to call legal aid and inform them of the situation I was in. She further stated that the lawyer I had was notorious for appearing in court intoxicated. She said it kind of hush hush as she really wasn't supposed to discuss it. I made a phone call from my cell phone and the woman in the office picked another lawyer for me.

In the court room I went with this new lawyer and needless to say he was even worse, we left the court room without the judge hearing my case and it as adjourned. I also did not have access to my children meaning I couldn't talk to them on the phone nor could I visit them I was fuming mad.

I sat down beside this new lawyer, and soon realized he was an asshole. Legal Aid doesn't allow them to bill very much and let's just say I resided in Abbotsford and it is crack central and many people lose their children due to drug addiction. Although my case was completely different let's just say this lawyer continuously interrupted me, and had a hate on for me from the minute I met him.

Every time I called him he would yell at me and claim I'm accusing him of this that and everything else. This guy was a pampas ass. So I decided to represent myself, after all who knows the Community Family Services Act better than myself, as I had researched the Act for the writing of this book.

Having my children removed from my care really made me put things in prospective, actually it made me put my entire life in prospective. When your children are taken from you from strangers it is scary. The overwhelming sense of emotions is very overpowering at times. I believe that it could make even the most level headed non emotional person emotional. I also believe that it could make a person do things that they most normally would never do. The thoughts that have ran through my head since the children were apprehended were "I want to kill the neighbors", "How dare they ever make a false report against me", to well the social workers will figure it out and know that I haven't abused the girls. They will also understand that I am not as bad as these people are claiming. What a farce. At least I know that's how I feel. I went to every person imaginable to try to sort the sordid mess that I was in out. I started to do this prior to the apprehension because I knew it was coming. Unfortunately I was gifted with a psychic ability to know things before they happen. Usually though I don't self predict meaning it doesn't involve my own life. Unfortunately in this case I have had predictions all the way through. I knew on the 27th of June four days prior to my girls being removed that my girls were going to be apprehended. I knew because of what was going on around me. I had the neighbor threaten to make false reports, and to beat me up, I had my other neighbor the one that I reported to child protection services also threatening me. I had a social worker on the 28th of June two days prior to the apprehension threaten to remove my kids if I continued with my complaint. So needless to say when they arrived at the house to remove the girls I was not surprised given everything that I had been through over the course of the previous three days.

I tried to make every attempt to stop this from happening, I guess I tried to change what I knew was about to happen. I couldn't for whatever reason I was not able to change it. Although I had already had conversations with the complaint resolution representative for the Ministry of Children & Families, and even with them informing me that they would not remove based on this, the girls were in actual fact removed.

I started to think okay why am I hitting my rock bottom, such as I had sixteen years prior when I was an addict that was in active addiction. Could it be because I had to find god again. Could it be that I was meant to go to church again and surround myself with religious people. I truly don't know the answer to my own question but what I can say is this. I did pick up and went to church. In fact God began to work miracles in my life shortly after the apprehension of my girls. He started with surrounding me with Christians. I turned out I had a neighbor who was a worship pastor at a local church, as well as his wife was Christian. I truly didn't believe that they would want to help me through this horrific situation. It turned out that the pastors wife had heard the whole altercation with "LEANNE", and heard her threaten me. Perhaps she was meant to hear it. She also stayed with me during a five hour interview with the social workers.

However, I still was not sure of god's plan in my life. As I started to have suicidal feelings about four days after the girls were apprehended. Those feelings occur mostly at night in the late evening hours. Mainly because I can't handle being alone. Perhaps it's because I have periods of doubt. Every mother doubts their parenting abilities, it's a normal feeling. I love my girls with all my heart but sometimes I think back to myself that if I just hadn't made that report on the neighbor that the girls would never have been placed in foster care.